Praise for *The Nature of Business*

A timely, paradigm-shifting book, reframing how business can thrive in the challenging times ahead…a brave book and a must read for those seeking to make positive change happen in business and beyond.

— Hunter Lovins, President of Natural Capitalism Solutions
and Co-author, *Natural Capitalism*

Simply the best new book on business and management in many years!

— Hazel Henderson, D.Sc.Hon. FRSA, author, *Building A Win-Win World*
and other books, President, Ethical Markets Media (USA and Brazil)

A rich source of inspiration and practical advice, bound to become a reference for business leaders and those teaching students of business. It beautifully maps the transformative journey for today's and tomorrow's leaders.

— Dr. Monika Winn, Business Strategy and Sustainability Director,
Centre for Social and Sustainable Innovation
Peter B. Gustavson School of Business, University of Victoria

Finally a guide to take this to the next level!

— Gunter Pauli, Founder of ZERI & The Blue Economy

A refreshing practical manual to how we can all challenge and adjust our thinking and take some profound actions to make a difference.

— Dr Alan Knight OBE, Chairman of the Global Association
of Corporate Sustainability Officers

For organizational leaders, *The Nature of Business* represents a compelling invitation and a comprehensive map for the journey not only toward sustainability but toward 'thrivability.' Thoroughly researched, with bite-sized but powerful case studies sprinkled throughout, it sparks insights and ideas at every turn. For the survival of our species, my greatest hope is that leaders everywhere will embark on the journey Giles describes in this important book.

— Michelle Holliday, Principal of Cambium Consulting
and author of *Humanity 4.0*

It is clear that as business people we need another mind-set. One that challenges preconceptions and builds new models, freeing our businesses to become more resilient and able to thrive in a rapidly changing and resource-constrained world. Giles has drawn together a compelling read for anybody interested in creating a better future.

— Andy Wood, CEO of Adnams PLC

This book not only brings together the current best practice and analysis of transformational business, but also seeks to find solutions. Giles has for many years been an innovative thinker based squarely in business and this book demonstrates that thought leadership; the book leaves me thinking much more clearly and feeling inspired to transform.

— Paul Drukman, CEO of The International Integrated Reporting Council

In times when business leaders are struggling with volatility and uncertainty about the future of their organizations, Giles Hutchins lays out a path for transformational change. Giles guides us to the essence of the role of business in society. By closing each module with a set of pertinent and personal questions, *The Nature of Business* is not just a very entertaining read, but also a redoubtable sparring partner. A must-read for everyone involved in the business of the future...and aren't we all?

— Mick Bremans, Chairman, Ecover

There is an energy, a pulse, a reverberating urgency that calls us to reflect and then take action in this book.... This book scores a line in the sand and invites us to step across, raise our voices, become visible, and engage. Now, and for all time.

— Tim Macartney, Director of Embercombe and author of *Finding Earth, Finding Soul*

Business faces enormous disruptive challenges in the next decade. For businesses to thrive in face of these pressures they must first protect nature, then learn from it and finally immerse themselves seamlessly with natural systems. Giles has found an elegant, engaging way of helping businesses to ask how they will do this.

— Mike Barry, Head of Sustainable Business, Marks & Spencer

We are creatures not cogs, and our ability to slough off the old certainties enforced by the clock and the conveyor belt are testament to a new movement in which business will be increasingly developed on biological lines, instilling resilience and adaptability rather than command control rigidity. These are exciting times, and the roar you hear in the background is of dinosaurs howling at a meteor crossing the night sky. This book is important for anyone seeking a roadmap to the future.

— Tim Smit, Founder of The Eden Project

Under the inspirational guidance of Giles we pioneered the 'firm of the future' approach and engaged our clients and partners on this exploratory path to a more sustainable and agile business ecosystem. This book will be an inspiration to the leaders of the future and I highly recommend it to anyone ready to be inspired by nature.

— Marianne Hewlett. Senior Vice President, Atos International

The NATURE of BUSINESS

Redesign for Resilience

Giles Hutchins

new society
PUBLISHERS

This book is dedicated to
Nature and her enchanting wisdom.

Also to
Star, Diana, Pip, Phil and Denise
for their unwavering support.

First published in the UK in 2012 by Green Books Ltd,
Dartington Space, Dartington Hall, Totnes, Devon TQ9 6EN

Copyright © 2013 Giles Hutchins. All rights reserved.

Cover design: Jayne Jones
Cover image © iStock (John Woodcock)

Printed in Canada. First printing March 2013

Paperback ISBN: 978-0-86571-737-4   eISBN: 978-1-55092-535-7

Inquiries regarding requests to reprint all or part of *The Nature of Business*
should be addressed to New Society Publishers at the address below.

To order directly from the publishers,
please call toll-free (North America) 1-800-567-6772,
or order online at www.newsociety.com

Any other inquiries can be directed by mail to:

New Society Publishers
P.O. Box 189, Gabriola Island, BC V0R 1X0, Canada
(250) 247-9737

LIBRARY AND ARCHIVES CANADA CATALOGUING IN PUBLICATION

Hutchins, Giles
The nature of business : redesign for resilience / Giles Hutchins.

Includes bibliographical references and index.
ISBN 978-0-86571-737-4

1. Organizational change — Environmental aspects.   2. Social
responsibility of business.   I. Title.

HD60.H88 2013   658.4'06   C2012-907434-9

New Society Publishers' mission is to publish books that contribute in fundamental
ways to building an ecologically sustainable and just society, and to do so with the
least possible impact on the environment, in a manner that models this vision. We
are committed to doing this not just through education, but through action. The
interior pages of our bound books are printed on Forest Stewardship Council®-
registered acid-free paper that is 100% **post-consumer recycled** (100% old growth
forest-free), processed chlorine free, and printed with vegetable-based, low-VOC
inks, with covers produced using FSC®-registered stock. New Society also works to
reduce its carbon footprint, and purchases carbon offsets based on an annual audit
to ensure a carbon neutral footprint. For further information, or to browse our
full list of books and purchase securely, visit our website at: www.newsociety.com

Contents

Acknowledgments

> We cannot do great things,
> only small things with great love.
> — **Mother Teresa**

I get by with a little help from my friends. In fact, I could argue that I get by with a little help from everyone and everything I interact with, friend or foe (if there is such), as I learn as best I can from each interaction. This book has been co-inspired and co-created through many life experiences, relationships and interconnections — too many to mention here.

I specifically mention here people who have co-created in the making of this book:

Denise DeLuca — BCI and SB 3000
Andy Middleton — BCI and TYF
Eric Dargent — BCI and One Planet MBA
Louise Carver — BCI and Natures Festival
Michael Edwards — BCI and IndigeNouse
And others in BCI (Polly, Belina, Nigel, Victoria, George, Michael)
Peter Redstone — Barefoot Thinking
Tony, Emma, Luisa and the rest of the crew at Tomorrow's Company
Nick Bellorini — the editor
Bruce Lipton — author and all-round force for good
Paul Francis — Shamanic Therapy
Alfred Schmits — The Conscious Company
Tim Macartney — Director of Embercombe
Sally Hill — WWF Australia
Trisha Comrie — Be The Change symposium

J-P and Sally Jeanrenaud—WWF International and Exeter University

John, Amanda, Stacey, Alethea, Bee, Hamish and the team at Green
Books

Andy Wood—Managing Director, Adnams

Mick Bremans—Chairman, Ecover

Eileen Donnely and Nick Fox—Virgin Management Ltd

Marianne Hewlett—Senior Vice-President, Atos

Prakash Tewari—Managing Trustee, Tata Power

Anant Nadkarni—Vice-President, Tata Group Corporate
Sustainability

Monique Simmons—Head of Innovation, Royal Botanic
Gardens, Kew

Mike Saunders—Head of Digital Media, Royal Botanic Gardens, Kew

Ingrid, EJ and the rest of the team at New Society Publishers

Preface

A paradigm is a constellation of concepts,
values, perceptions and practices
shared by a community, which forms
a particular vision of reality.
— Fritjof Capra

Human science disciplines over the past four decades have been pre-occupied with the way these concepts, values and practices shape how we see ourselves in the world and the stories we tell ourselves. If these stories are taken for granted and never questioned, then they tend to be reproduced over and over again. The social and scientific revolutions in modern, early modern and even ancient ages have left their legacies with the modern mind, and ultimately the "stories" it unwittingly defaults to. For example, the early modern period, in the Renaissance and the Enlightenment, saw major revelations in scientific discovery and philosophy from Copernicus, Galileo, Newton, Descartes and Darwin, which greatly influenced the modern Western view of the human in the wider cosmos and universe. Man became a powerful external actor, disconnected from the very fabric of the natural systems of which he had previously been a part.

Interestingly, these events were both profoundly liberating for human societies and also enormously disenchanting. Other major transformations in rapid industrialization and urbanization continued to reinforce a sense of separation between society and nature, human and non-human worlds, lived-in lands and pristine Edens. It is arguably this sense of separation that has enabled society to capitalize on the fruits of science, industry and global economics. Conversely, it is also what underwrites the parallel dysfunction and destruction of our social and ecological systems.

The ecological, social and economic crisis now upon us is as much a crisis of spirit as it is a crisis of resources. Indeed, part of the crisis of spirit is because modern society and industry tend to perceive the Earth as a set of resources, and value it as such. What scope is there for this paradigm to change in order to perceive the Earth as an animate, living system in which humans play a constructive, not destructive, part?

We may see how the politics of human–nature relations connects with the politics of human knowledge systems. Increasingly we are asking what an overly mechanistic and reductive logic obscures from view and how it conditions our knowledge. Other forms of knowledge of nature exist outside of a modern Western philosophy (for example, those related to holistic science and practices by traditional cultures).

Advances in science have allowed humans to manipulate, manage, interpret, document and now literally create life with technology (with developments in synthetic biology). Science in its mechanistic form has revealed an ecological crisis, but it is doubtful that it is wholly equipped to reverse this crisis. The solutions are social, cultural and economic, not just technical. This perspective doesn't propose to undo science, yet it suggests that it should be reflective of its own limits. It is equally crucial to pose challenges such as "how far," "how fast," "which way," "who says" and "why," not merely a question of balancing a "pro" and "anti" position.

The same reflexivity is just as important in business. Since what is required is a radically new way of doing business — one that honors and values intrinsically (rather than financially) the global nexus of social and ecological systems — we could also argue that this is only one (yet important) factor within a much wider transition in collective consciousness. In 2010 The Royal Society of Arts (RSA), a British Enlightenment institution founded in 1754, coined their new strapline: *a 21st-century enlightenment*. Matthew Taylor, the RSA Director, proposes that the core ideals, values and norms that the initial Enlightenment enabled may no longer be adequate or "fit for purpose" for the contemporary challenges society faces. In order to live differently, he argues, we must think differently, and this relates to the way that we see ourselves in the world. Change may not be so much an act of will as a consequence of a subtler shift in fundamental scientific, cultural, philosophical and even spiritual factors. The push-and-pull forces for such a shift are as likely to be a series of positive and negative cyclic feedbacks across the social, technological, scientific and political fields, in much the same way as they have been during historical transitions.

If these inclinations do point toward something meaningfully transformative with respect to the nature of reality, ways of being and collective thinking, then the question is this: how do we begin to interpret, explore and promote radical thinking in the fields in which we work, be they business, education, environmental governance or social policy? Cultural communicators in diverse fields and institutions seem to point in the direction of radical transformation in some shape or form.

There are many profound questions facing us. This book touches on some of them — such as the relationship between human nature and nature in a business context — yet it does not try to answer them; rather, it explores the challenges business is now faced with, the limitations of our prevailing business paradigm, and the approaches to help individuals and organizations positively adapt in the face of these challenging times.

The nature of transformation and shifting paradigms is complex, of course, yet it is hoped that this book picks out salient aspects of this underlying complexity and presents them in an easily digestible way for the reader. If the reader desires to understand more, I hope this book will act as a channel into a deeper debate.

Through the lenses of nature and human nature, peppered with examples and quotes, this book explores the transformation of organizations and how they can best embark on a journey toward becoming more "fit for purpose" for the world we now live in. In focusing on organizations, it also touches on people as individuals and as groups, providing positive ways forward for people in business (and beyond) to start realizing a better future for ourselves, and for the organizations and communities we seek to serve.

Introduction

No change without action;
no action without thought.

— Anonymous

This book is intended for those interested in exploring and undertaking transformational change within organizations: leaders, managers, change agents, academics and entrepreneurs. A variety of ideas and concepts extracted from theories relevant to organizational transformation are put forward here — of which some have been applied to business for a while now, and others are more recent arrivals. While rooting concepts in thought and theory is sensible, thought without action and interaction (like theory without practice) is ultimately fruitless.

It is important that the book walks its own talk, so to speak, and so helps provoke thought, action and interaction in you, the reader. And so it has been laid out in modules (rather than chapters), with each module unfolding important aspects (challenges and opportunities) of the transformational journey, while helping to prompt right action toward positive transformation.

Each module is framed with an executive summary at the start, setting out the main points covered in the module at a glance, and each ends with interactive questions for you to engage with. It is the thinking and then doing that is important here — not getting the right answer, but the initiation of thought and then deed. Tools, concepts, references, questions and insights into ways of sensing and responding are offered to help you challenge and embrace the opportunity of making positive change happen in your organization. Many concepts and approaches are, by their very nature, work in progress, continuously emerging to new levels and only alive when being experienced in practice; hence it is hoped that the reader engages with the questions at the end of each module with a desire to explore, share, co-create and add to this emergence.

We live in very interesting, challenging and yet exciting times, full of opportunity to make positive change. The most important part of any transformation is initiating it, getting the ball rolling, and then using the momentum of change to drive forward the transformation, with right principles, values and signposts to navigate the transformative path ahead. With that in mind, please visit the website below, where you can engage further with the challenges we face, and where you will find additional information and inspiration.

Let's make change happen and have some creative fun in the process. Join the debate at businessinspiredbynature.com/natureofbusiness (for online discussions by module) and thenatureofbusiness.org (the blog for the book audience and co-creators in the field of Business Inspired By Nature).

Transformational Times Call for Transformational Change

> At times of great winds, some build bunkers,
> while others build windmills.
>
> — Ancient Chinese proverb

EXECUTIVE SUMMARY

- Business has a major impact on all spheres of life.
- Business behavior is much affected by the prevailing business paradigm, which is still being reinforced today by publications and management education.
- We do not need to be bound by mindsets and mentalities about business that are no longer fit for purpose.
- A more balanced, interconnected understanding of business aids positive adaptation in an increasingly volatile business environment.
- Business can deliver value for itself while benefiting society and the environment; this is good business sense.
- Each and every one of us in business has the potential to be a force for good, thus helping ourselves and our organizations to survive and thrive.

Business of today

Since the Second World War, the West has witnessed unprecedented economic growth. Emerging economies too have followed suit, some now ranked as the top economic powers of the world. Industrialization, technological advancement, economies of scale and increasingly efficient approaches to profit maximization have led to what we see today—the good and the not so good.

We live in a world of paradoxes. While the drive for economic growth is often rooted in a desire to improve the well-being of the stakeholders that the organization or economy seeks to serve, there have been winners and losers. There have been great benefits and also great costs.

The currently prevailing view of the purpose of business is this: to provide goods and services to meet the perceived needs of the customer in order to generate profit for shareholders. The more the customer consumes, the better, as more goods and services are sold, and hence more profit gained. This is what we refer to today as "consumerism." Consumption-based growth has become the driving force of economic growth, which in turn provides employment, providing income for consumers to consume more, in turn fuelling more economic growth. This prevailing business view is incomplete in at least two aspects.

First, business is primarily focused on providing ever more goods and services to generate more profit. This profit is determined by an economic value (and cost), disconnected from social and environmental value (and cost), incurred through sourcing, production and consumption. There are a number of "externalities" that are not incorporated within the economic value and cost (the organization's balance sheet does not include a wide range of social and environmental costs and benefits). In other words, social and environmental value (the benefits and costs to all stakeholders) are not included within the current prevailing measurement of economic value. The consumer's price paid does not reflect true, complete value. Nor do the producer's costs incurred reflect true, complete cost. Hence, the prevailing approach to value, cost and profit is incomplete.

Second, the goal of business is to satisfy the needs of the customer. In so doing, the clever business mind seeks to encourage the desires of the customer so that their needs best align to the products and services of that business. This would seem sensible business. Hence, business invests in marketing, communications, media and advertising to help generate a demand for the goods and services it produces. In turn, the needs of the customer (the human) become influenced and encouraged by business. Does it matter if the influenced needs of the human no longer contribute to their present and future well-being? If the human consumes the product or service due to a perceived need and feels sat-isfied for a short period, then is it good business? Alas, we develop an economy that encourages human needs that are not always (perhaps seldom) aligned to the real well-being of the human. More sobering is that this can affect social and cultural norms by encouraging the pursuit of perceived needs and desires over the pursuit of betterment through values, character and wisdom. Hence, the prevailing approach to need (and well-being) is incomplete.

The vast majority of global human ingenuity is currently focused on generating incomplete value for incomplete needs. This incomplete-ness, I would argue, greatly contributes to the amount of trouble and strife in the world today.

It is also worth noting here the role of money in our current para-digm. Money is an excellent transaction medium. Money as a trans-action medium provides "I owe you" promises to pay between parties. Bizarrely, lending institutions (banks) have the right to issue new money (new "promises to pay") based on the debt facility (which can be up to 90 percent of the original "promise to pay"). This is known as fractional reserve banking; it is the most common form of banking in the world today, ensuring the broad money supply of most countries is far larger than the amount of base money created by each country's central bank.[1] And so money creates debt, which creates new money, which in turn creates more debt and more new money, and so on. The more money there is, the more debt there is. Lending institutions have been creating debt and money in a way that is no longer connected to value creation, which of course undermines the value of money, which in turn undermines the health of the economy, as it relies on it for value exchange.

As economies struggle, many look to stimulate more consump-tion — cheaper credit is the panacea. Encouraging more of the same is flawed. Bold decisions are needed that explore how long-lasting, wholesome economic activity can move us beyond the current conun-drum. Many senior economists are patently aware that stimulating yet more consumption through yet more debt is exacerbating the funda-mental economic problems we face. For example, Sir Mervyn King, the Governor of The Bank of England, stated in October 2011 that "unless overspending by Western economies was curbed it would bring about an ever-larger debt crisis that would mean much lower long-term growth rates." The root cause of the debt crisis threatening major Western economies, he said, was a long period of "unsustainably high levels of consumption," in which governments, companies and individuals spent more than they earned.[2]

It seems a harsh generalization to characterize business as a whole as excessively exploitative and greedy, and of course we know there are many in business that are neither. Also, we know of many products and services that aspire to providing real well-being for the customer. This book highlights some such examples. Indeed, it is perhaps understandable how we got into this prevailing paradigm. Only a hundred years ago (just a couple of generations), the world was viewed as an untapped source of goodness. Commerce and industry flourished by exploiting seemingly limitless natural resources.

Since the Industrial Revolution, we have achieved great feats of economic, social and technological advancement for which, as a species, we can be proud. Yet the challenges (and opportunities) now facing our businesses, economies and societies are all too apparent. These include:

- volatile input costs
- volatile prices
- volatile consumer buying patterns
- increasing complexity and risk in supply chains
- changing demographics, world population shifts
- shift to a multipolar world
- increasing socioeconomic/political tensions
- increasing scarcity of finite natural resources
- increasing propensity of food and water shortages
- increasing frequency of natural disasters and epidemics
- climate change
- peak oil, peak elements, and so on
- ocean acidification and dead zones
- rapid decline in biodiversity
- increasing inequality

- rising world poverty
- increasing mental health issues and stress-related illnesses
- exponential growth in population and consumption rates.

So what has all this got to do with business and business paradigms?

First, it is our current business paradigm that has exacerbated the imbalances, tensions and volatility we face today. As Albert Einstein observed: "We cannot solve the problems in the world with the same level of thinking that brought them about in the first place."[3] To operate in the world we now live in, we need fresh approaches to businesses that are fit for the present and future.

Second, good business is fundamentally about seeking out opportunities for value creation, not about trying to get something for nothing. As our social, economic and environmental landscapes become ever more volatile, business approaches need to adapt and evolve to optimize the opportunities for value creation.

Third, in the words of Paul Hawken, "Business and industry is the only institution that is large enough, pervasive enough and powerful enough to lead humankind out of this mess."[4] Therefore, the reevaluation and transformation of our business paradigm is fundamental to the successful evolution, not only of business, but of our species as a whole.

In times of pressing challenges, in this perfect storm of social, economic and environmental volatility, it requires great courage to break rank from a paradigm that is ingrained in our business mindset. Transformational times call for transformational change. Businesses that wish to thrive and survive in these volatile times must transform themselves from what I will call "firms of the past" to "firms of the future," so that instead of responding in incomplete ways to these pressing challenges, they anticipate and embrace change in the most successful way.

The good news is that there are courageous, bold people at all levels in organizations across the board that recognize the need to transform. Unsurprisingly, like any step change in evolution, the herd are fearfully holding on for dear life to a business paradigm that has now "expired." Let us first explore this prevailing "expired" paradigm — the firm of the past — which is based on conventional thinking, and organizational characteristics that we are all familiar with, yet which are no longer suitable for the world we now inhabit. As Jack Welch (former CEO of General Electric) put it: "When change within a business is slower than that without, you're in real trouble."[5]

The firm of the past

The firm of the past is resolute in its goal — "to maximise shareholder return." Over the last few decades, shareholders (and the investment market) have in the main become more interested in short-term returns. The goal of the firm of the past has thus increasingly become one of short-term profit, utilizing two main levers: cost reduction (bottom-line management) and value enhancement (top-line growth).

Values and behaviors that assist the goal are encouraged; ones that do not are eliminated. The firm of the past is based on a "command-and-control" philosophy. Management and governance are fundamental to ensuring effective operations within the firm of the past. Without such "carrot and stick" management structures (with all the tricks of the trade that are used to influence), people and processes could not be driven continuously toward ever-increasing short-term profits.

Economies of scale and industrialization have been the main drivers for value-enhancement and cost reduction in a firm of the past: enhancing the bottom line through sweating of assets and reducing unit cost of production, while increasing turnover and market share where possible. Increased market share brings with it economies of scale, monopolistic benefits, and brand enhancement associated with "bigger is better and safer" for customers, partners and investors. Merger and acquisition activity over the last few decades has thus been increasing, being viewed as the best way to protect and enhance shareholder returns. Also, acquisitive strategies seem like easier shortcuts to improved returns than through organic growth, which can be time-consuming and challenging.

Bottom-line management and top-line growth, while two sides of the same business coin, require different approaches, often attracting different mentalities. Bottom-line management is rooted in efficiency gains, approached through tight governance, risk management, quality control and operational excellence approaches (for example, Six

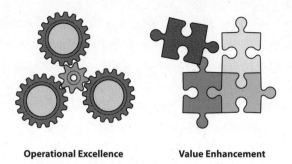

Operational Excellence   **Value Enhancement**

Figure 1. Two sides of the business coin.

Sigma[6]). Top-line growth is rooted in value-enhancement gains through improved sales win rates, higher product differentiation, higher brand value, higher margin contracts, improved goodwill and innovation, among other things. The former, operational excellence, is more of a science (measuring, monitoring, reducing, controlling); the latter, value-enhancement, is more of an art (brand recognition, client relations, perceived product differentiation, empathic sales relationships, creativity through innovation).

Executives in the firm of the past tend to be measured on short-term quantifiable improvements where possible. Executives often move positions after a couple of years in post having shown results against these short-term quantifiable measures, referred to as key performance indicators (KPIs). Such KPIs tend to be cascaded down through the hierarchy of governance within the organization. Hence, executives delegate to lower-ranking subordinates within the governance structure, who in turn delegate to the "shop-floor" operatives. Each level of governance is focused on the short-term results, with consistency of behavior being managed through these measures in a "carrot and stick" fashion. The person who achieves "the numbers" gains the "carrot": bonus, pay raise, increased status, promotion. The person who fails to achieve "the numbers" is given the "stick": loss of bonus, substandard performance rating, reduced status, possible loss of employment. The executive who excels in achieving personal targets, while underperforming on team or group targets, is viewed as "high-performing" compared with an executive who excels in team or group targets while underperforming on personal targets. The executive who understands how to manage "the numbers" consistently to forecast is often rewarded with senior executive positions, sometimes even CEO, as the ability to manage consistently by "the numbers" is seen as critical in the firm of the past. Managers are appointed as leaders due to their ability to rationalize, control and de-risk, rather than their empathic and visionary leadership in challenging times.

Hence, the business paradigm of the firm of the past reinforces its own mentality through this focus on managing rather than leading, on personal excellence rather than team excellence, on risk mitigation rather than exploring new ways of operating to create additional value. Unfortunately, this business paradigm makes a rod for its own back, and life within the firm of the past becomes increasingly stressful as demands for improving on last quarter's earnings endlessly continue, while relentless bottom-line management results in reduced investment in value-enhancement capabilities. Ever-decreasing capability of long-term growth is the cost incurred for singular focus on short-term profit maximization — focusing on today's harvest at the expense of sowing fewer seeds for the future. Sooner or later the future becomes the present, and it becomes harder and harder to maximize short-term shareholder returns with this business mentality.

In the firm of the past, questions like "whom is this organization serving?" are met with rolling eyes and responses of "it's the shareholders, of course!" Dare one ask who the shareholders are, or what their underlying motive for the long-term success of the organization is? It is this "short-term shareholder return is king" mentality, reinforced by a fixation with "numbers, numbers, numbers," that typifies the firm of the past. Business needs to rationalize and quantify, while also qualifying and contextualizing. Focusing on one at the expense of the other is not a recipe for success.

Reductionism and systems thinking

Neuroscientist Iain McGilchrist explores left-brain dominance in our Western culture.[7] The left brain, according to McGilchrist's findings, focuses on parts of the problem, decontextualizing and abstracting the problem in a closed system. This, of course, helps us to analyze and find a solution to that problem. But this is a solution in its isolated closed system, not in a living, emergent, volatile business environment. The right brain is what interconnects, provides living world context, views things in an open system and develops a broad understanding. It is both the knowledge of the parts (left brain) and wisdom of the whole (right brain) that we need for complete and proper problem understanding and correct solution creation. To quote Einstein, "The intuitive mind is a sacred gift and the rational mind is a faithful servant."[8] For McGilchrist, "we have created a society that honors the servant but has forgotten the gift."[9]

Left-brain dominance has roots in a reductionist philosophy that came long before today's prevailing business paradigm. Descartes and Newton, among others, helped sow the seeds of reductionism: the view that the behavior of the whole system can be explained in terms of the behavior of their constituent parts. This atomization of complex,

Figure 2. Systems thinking.
Source: Reproduced with permission from Systems Thinking International (www.sys-think.com).

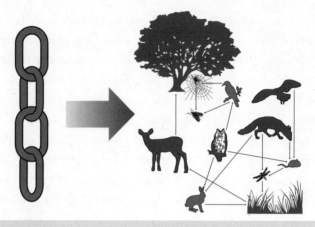

Figure 3. Linear to interconnected.

interconnected systems greatly assisted our understanding of science and the development of technologies. Management and monitoring approaches have brought great strides in efficiency of operations, aided our understanding of the subsystem parts of business, and helped us to analyze, quantify and control. However, a focus on measuring atomized parts of the system needs to be adequately balanced with an understanding of the interrelationship of the parts and the wider system context. Intuitively, we know that life is not simply made up of building blocks that can be rationalized, measured and monitored for improved efficiency and effectiveness.

Systems thinking is thinking in terms of interconnections, patterns and processes rather than stovepipes and separate units. It recognizes the interconnected nature of business and wider life, and views the whole system as greater than the sum of its parts. While reductionism helps the understanding of isolated parts, systems thinking helps us understand and deal with complexity and change.

In these ever-complex and interconnected times, systems thinking is increasingly being applied to business challenges such as strategy development, process re-engineering, team dynamics and organizational learning.[10]

It is our prevailing reductionist approach to science, technology and business that has encouraged us to see ourselves as separate from nature, and to view the world around us as something to be analyzed and over-exploited for our own wants and needs, with scant regard for the consequences. Here lies insight into some of the root causes of our problems facing us today in business and beyond: an unbalanced approach to quantifying without also qualifying, and reducing without also understanding the whole and interconnected parts.

Many humans have behaved, and continue to behave, in a balanced and life-encompassing way, which gives us great hope that it is not our being human that is the problem, just our prevailing understanding and level of awareness. Yet the sobering fact of the matter is that our current business approach (and its immense power to fuel problems as well as implement solutions) is neither balanced nor life-encompassing; it is reductionist and anthropocentric in its belief and behavior. The Be the Change group has noted that:

> According to a majority of the world's experts, there is now over-whelming evidence that our modern society is headed for a ca-tastrophe. Leading scientists are telling us that the impact of our industrial system, and the sudden expansion of humanity's abil-ity to harvest the common bounty of our planet for short-term gain, may actually be upsetting the balance of our highly complex and fragile web of life.

It is as if we are living inside of a dream, sleepwalking toward oblivion, while self-serving, short-sighted interests encourage our slumber with managed news, celebrity culture and other weapons of mass distrac-tion.[11]

Time to transform

As a result of its focus on operational excellence, economies of scale and predictable returns on investment, the firm of the past is a well-managed organization, with many attributes that business minds can be proud of. The firm of the past is independent, stable, efficient, risk-aware, con-trolled, self-focused, competitive, driven and quantifiable. Alas, these attributes are no longer "good enough" on their own for an organiza-tion operating in a business environment that is increasingly volatile, impossible to predict or control, complex, open and interconnected. These are the times within which we now operate, and the level of volatility is only set to increase for the foreseeable future. The firm of the past, with all its strengths, is no longer fit for purpose.

In the words of Dawn Vance, Director of Global Logistics at Nike:

> Organizations have three options:
> 1. Hit the wall
> 2. Optimize and delay hitting the wall
> 3. Redesign for resilience.[12]

Organizations, executives, employees and investors who hold on tightly to these out-dated business approaches that served us well in the past will find life harder and harder, swimming against an ever-increasing torrent of dynamic change. It is organizations and individuals that recognize the need to adapt and transform that shall flourish by pursuing opportunities within turbulence.

> Seeing a turbulent world through threat-tinted glasses invites the dysfunctions of threat rigidity — centralized control, limited experimentation, and focus on existing resources — that stymies the pursuit of opportunity.
> — DONALD SULL[13]

Business has learned a considerable amount from the past, with the positive attributes of the firm of the past remaining important as we shift forward to a new paradigm that balances quantity with quality, operational excellence with value creation, the short term with the long term, self-focus with system-focus, and stability with dynamism.

The business environment ahead

There is a multitude of reasons driving increased volatility over the next few years; let's explore five factors that are particularly pertinent to our business environment:

- globalization
- digitization
- responsible business

+ pressure on finite natural resources
+ business risk from "black swan" events.

Globalization

The world of business is becoming increasingly interconnected. We export, import, fly, ship and truck more materials and goods between geographical locations than ever before, and the trend is increasing. Business has been talking about globalization for the last couple of decades, and now it is upon us, evidenced by goods and services across all spectra being sold and delivered across all regions in the world. No country or market remains untouched by globalization (although a few exceptions try to minimize its effects, such as Bhutan and Cuba). All parts of the world are accessible to global market forces. We have become a global village of trading organizations with interconnected capital and money markets. Shocks in one part of the world send ripples throughout the whole interconnected world economy.

Globalization's antithesis is localization. The two do not have to be mutually exclusive; in fact, finding the mix, the harmonic balance, is key for our global community's future viability and success. Globalization that seeks to destroy local expertise, local diversity and the ability of local communities to provide basic essentials for themselves is a globalization that shall erode local and, in turn, global resilience, leading to its own demise.

Digitization

The all-pervasive Internet makes the "always on, working any time, any place, anywhere" environment a reality—the new world of working. Again, business has been talking about concepts such as the digital age, e-commerce, open source and virtualization for some years. Now it is upon us, it is a very real part of our economy and society and only set to increase in terms of its use and coverage. Whether it be social media helping to aid civil unrest, going viral with government secrets or exposing suspect business behavior, digitization is opening up traditional boundaries between work and home life, between private and public. How and what businesses communicate is increasingly important. It is becoming more difficult and expensive to keep business behavior private. Hence, "walking the talk" is increasingly important, as marketing and promotional communications that do not stack up to the reality of actual business behavior can be mercilessly exposed for the untruths they seek to obscure.

Digitization also encourages disruptive technologies to emerge that challenge the status quo of business; for example, co-creation open-source technology environments, where people across different geographies can collaborate, share ideas and innovate together. Such open-source environments challenge business norms of intellectual property (IP) rights and patents. For example Nike, Best Buy and Creative Commons formed GreenXchange, where innovations are shared in a community-based knowledge-transfer environment with patent-pool communities and public licensing for patents.[14]

Responsible business

The interconnectedness driven by globalization and digitization brings with it the need for a business to be smarter, or simply more transparent and truthful. Once truth is sought, it ultimately needs to be the whole truth and nothing but the truth—hence, business models that perform against KPIs (Key Performance Indicators) that do not measure the whole truth will need to explain, and live up to, their path toward measuring the whole truth. Businesses that truly walk the talk shine out and differentiate themselves against those that are merely manipulating stories to make their behavior appear wholesome, when in fact it is not. It will be in the organization's best long-term interest to be a responsible business, a business that understands its costs and benefits to the society and environment within which it operates, a business that seeks to take responsibility for its actions and interactions while generating value for its stakeholders. This drive toward responsible business asks the firm of the past uncomfortable questions about its business paradigm. Businesses able to find solutions to these uncomfortable questions can reap the rewards that good business sense brings (brand enhancement, customer loyalty, employee engagement, etc.). Firms of the past that do not change their ways will be hunted out by the seekers of truth through the all-pervasive Internet. Businesses and executives unable to understand and plan for the transformation toward responsible business will become old news. They need to adapt or die, with truth being the judge.

> Child labor in Nike's factories and supply chain was publicly exposed in the 1990s, which led to the brand being badly damaged and profits adversely impacted. Nike sought to adapt and transform toward a more responsible and transparent business. Part of that transformation is its "Considered" range of products, which considers the social and environmental impacts incurred in sourcing and production, providing information to the customer on aspects such as toxicity, waste and sustainable materials. Nike's goal is to have 100 percent of its products "considered" by 2020. In embarking on this transformation, Nike has strengthened its brand, gained a far better grip on its operations, improved collaboration with its partners, built resilience into its business and increased its ability to attract and retain talent through a values-based culture. Responsible business is good business.

Pressure on finite natural resources

The world is finite and, except for solar energy and the odd meteor, is pretty much a closed system, materially. We have to make the best use of the natural resources we have on our planet. Over the last few decades we have pillaged our natural assets at an alarming rate. Living off assets, rather than income, is short-sighted. As Mohandas K. Gandhi said: "Earth provides enough to satisfy every man's need, but not every man's greed."[15]

All our materials, products, food and shelter originate from the natural world. The natural world has been recycling its nutrients very well for billions of years. We have yet to get our collective heads around how to recycle and reuse effectively; business acumen and creative potential has not been encouraged and rewarded adequately to get to grips with recycling and reuse on an appropriate scale. In fact, our current business paradigm actually encourages and rewards the opposite — growth based on increased consumption of natural resources, with waste seen as an inconvenient by-product. We continue to extract, heat, beat, treat, transport, consume and then dump masses of natural resources as waste each year, while exploiting our natural resources beyond their natural carrying capacity, in the name of business. Business efficiency and operational excellence ought to have ensured the greatest longevity of nature's resources, and in turn the longevity of the living systems and organizations that they support. Instead, efficiency gains have been siphoned off to achieve short-term profit maximization for increased shareholder returns, in turn exploiting the very asset base that creates value for future profit. This is hardly good business sense. According to Mervyn E. King, Chairman of the Global Reporting Initiative (not to be confused with the Bank of England Governor quoted earlier):

> Since the days of the industrial revolution, companies have conducted business on two false assumptions, namely that the earth has infinite resources and has an infinite capacity to absorb waste. In fact, the earth has finite resources and the landfills from this "Take, Make, Waste" philosophy, both on land and in the oceans, have resulted in the toxification of the land and waters of the earth. The planet is in crisis, as we have reached ecological overshoot, which means that we have used and continue to use the natural resources of planet Earth faster than nature can regenerate them.[16]

It is not simply our atmosphere that we pollute causing climate change, but our oceans, our rivers, our landscapes, our soils. This prevailing business paradigm is having immense impact on our real ability to do good business on this planet (as well as massively impacting society and the natural environment). It is harder and harder to find reliable, secure, stably priced sources of basic commodities these days. Food, minerals, metals, fossil fuels and the like are all increasingly price-sensitive due to the immense pressure we have placed on natural resources due to over-exploitation and short-termism. Yet again our short-sighted business paradigm comes back to haunt us, as asset depletion leaves us with a massive debt to be settled with nature. Global Overshoot Day (the point in the year by which we have already consumed the amount our planet can provide for sustainably, which means living off the income rather than the asset base) in 2010 was August 21; of course, it's getting earlier and earlier each year.

Unlike the debt of a sovereign nation or bank, the debt we are accumulating with nature cannot be restructured or diluted through administration. There is no debt default with nature, no financial loophole or escape route; we must pay our dues. And that we shall.

In the "natural capitalism" model, put forward by Paul Hawken, Amory Lovins and Hunter Lovins, it is argued that just as the scarcity of human resources drove the logic of the first Industrial Revolution, so shall the scarcity of natural resources act as a catalyst for the next industrial revolution, which will be based on four strategies:

1. Radically increased resource productivity.
2. Redesign of business models and processes based on nature with closed loops and zero-waste.
3. Shifting from the sale of goods to the provision of services.
4. Reinvesting in natural and human capital.[17]

We touch on these points later in the book as they form part of what good can look like in business, and help provide a positive direction for business. As Richard Branson said:

> The great news is that looking at how we protect and harness our natural resources is the largest "great frontier" we will have in our lifetimes. If we get it right (which we can and must) this new frontier will create millions of new jobs, save money for existing businesses and propel us into a way of life that is far more harmonious with nature and prosperous for all.[18]

Business risk from "black swan" events

The risk organizations face due to unpredictable disruptions of large magnitude and consequence (referred to as "black swan" events by Nassim Taleb in his book *The Black Swan*[19]) increases as our business world becomes more interconnected, stressed and turbulent. Building resilience into the organization (through robustness and agility) helps the organization to absorb negative fallout while being best placed to act upon opportunities that arise from major disturbances. As the level of uncertainty increases, future scenario planning in business can help with the sensing and responding to market disruptions.

To summarize this opening module, our current prevailing approach to business has led us into the current reality of a debt-laden society, debt-laden economy and debt-laden environment. Business is part of the problem, yet business is also most definitely part of the solution.

Business is a powerful force for transformation; it is now time to make it a force for good. Each and every one of us in business has the potential to be a change agent for the positive adaptation that helps us as individuals, as organizations, as economies and as a global species. Each of us can freely choose to be part of the problem or part of the solution.

Questions

1   Is your organization aware of its social, environmental and economic impacts (whether positive or negative)? List them.

2. How many people could your organization affect directly? To calculate this number, add up the following (have an initial guess and then develop accuracy later).

    • How many customers do your products and services serve (e.g., per month/year)?

    • If you supply B2B, how many business customers do you have and approximately how many employees do they have? How many consumers do your business customers serve?

    • How many suppliers do you have? And how many employees do they have?

    • How many people work in your organization? (Note that you could increase this number by allowing for all these individuals' families.)

3. What are some of the key economic, social and environmental challenges/changes facing your organization now? Are there others that you anticipate emerging in the next five to ten years?

4. What do you think will happen if you and your organization ignore the volatility and dramatic changes that are occurring in the world today and in the foreseeable future?

5. How aware do you think most people in your organization are of these changes (and the challenges they represent)? What about senior management/business owners?

6. Who do you feel is responsible for driving the changes of the scale, scope and speed needed?

7. In your sphere of influence in your organization, are there actions you could take?

8. Are there examples in your organization of people taking proactive action in response to major economic, social and environmental challenges?

9. Do you personally believe that a business can simultaneously deliver value to itself while being a force for good for the community and the natural environment? If so, what might that look like? How might you make that work?

10. Does the firm-of-the-past approach to business relate to your organization in any way? What characteristics come to mind that are "firm of the past" in type? For example: hierarchical; siloed; risk-averse; quantity-focused; maximization-focused; short-term-focused; individual performance valued higher than team performance; the numbers come first, not the people; change-resistant; and so on.

11. What organizations does your company interrelate with in order to go about its business? What sort of relationship(s) does your company have with these other organizations? How would you quantify the relationship? How would you qualify the relationship?

12. Do you believe that all business relationships are fundamentally competitive? If so, do you also feel that all of your personal relationships are fundamentally competitive? Reflect on how, in your personal life, you derive value by focusing on others, and how focusing on others can bring value to you. Can you imagine applying this same approach to relationships in your professional life?

13. Is there potential to develop relationships with suppliers and/or partners to deliver much greater value for all? Where might be a good place to start?

Nature as Teacher

> He who is in harmony with Nature
> hits the mark without effort, and
> apprehends the truth without thinking.
>
> — **Confucius**

EXECUTIVE SUMMARY

:• We are part of nature, and so it makes sense to understand the constraints and organizing forces of nature.

:• Nature has been dealing with dynamic change for over 3.8 billion years, and is constantly perfecting approaches to survival and resilience that are relevant for organizations who wish to be resilient.

:• Successful adaptation and evolution in nature are less about competition and more about cooperation, networking and finding niches within ecosystems of relationships and resources.

:• Biomimicry and nature's principles can be applied to business transformation.

:• Aspects of nature provide insight for business resilience (e.g., swarm behavior, relationship types, ecosystem dynamics, emergence).

:• Reigniting our vital bond with nature provides inspiration from which business innovation can spawn.

:• It is fear of change and the unknown that inhibits our ability to positively adapt; "letting go" of that fear through courage is an important step toward successful adaptation.

This module explores nature's wisdom, while applying it to a business context. There is immense (seemingly limitless) depth and breadth to nature's wisdom. Salient aspects are covered in short sections within this module in a bite-sized way, hopefully providing appetite for the reader to undertake deeper examination and application.

Nature in context

First and foremost, we must recognize that we humans are a part of nature. We have unique qualities (which we shall explore in Module Five, Human Nature and Nurture), yet we are part of the interconnected, interdependent web of life.

Our current separated thinking and reductionist view of the world have encouraged an alienation from nature over recent years, leaving us unbalanced in our understanding of the real world — the world not just of stock-market trends and commodity prices, but also of soil and sea, of cycles and seasons, and of ecosystems and environments.

Our prevailing view of nature as a battleground of competing species, each fighting to survive, is a narrow view of a more complex picture. When Charles Darwin published his *The Origin of Species*, the phrase "survival of the fittest" was quickly co-opted and distorted by powerful elites to promote the idea that only the biggest, strongest and most powerful can survive. In reality, what Darwin found and described in his book was that those organisms with the greatest ability to adapt to their local environment — the "fittest" in the sense of the best fit — would survive when and where others would fail. He found that sensing, responding, adapting, and aligning with and within the local ecosystem were key to survival. Recent scientific discoveries, coupled with advances in systems thinking and quantum theory, continue to build on these findings, and uncover a more complex and complete view of nature, the workings of the universe and the evolution of life.

Over the last 3.8 billion years, nature has survived and flourished through times of radical change and disruption by dynamically networking and collaborating among species and throughout ecosystems. Competition and constraints help shape nature, yet it is collaboration and synergy — not competition — that are responsible for nature's sustained success. The species most able to survive and evolve are those most able to sense and respond, adapt and align, and work in partnership with and within their ecosystems. Diversity, flexibility and collaboration, we find, are core to the interwoven evolutionary journey of life — the driving forces that provide resilience within species and ecosystems.

> Popular wisdom holds that the fittest survive, the strongest, leanest, largest, perhaps meanest — whatever beats the competition. But in healthy, thriving natural systems it is actually the "fittingest" who thrive. Fitting-est implies an energetic and material engagement with place, and an interdependent relationship to it.
> — MICHAEL BRAUNGART AND WILLIAM MCDONOUGH[1]

Nature is a web of energized interconnections, a "dynamic non-equilibrium" of chaos within order, order within chaos. The same is true, of course, for humans and human nature, as we are a part of nature, while exhibiting our own profound uniqueness.

Whether it be cardiology, mental health, personal relationships or trading-floor behavior, the seemingly paradoxical juxtapositions of chaos and order abound. Though we find great comfort in order and the known, the deeper we explore the rhythms within our daily lives, the more we find that chaos and diversity are natural and healthy. Our ability to adapt and fully embrace life with its special spontaneity is what drives evolution. Fear of chaos and resistance to the unknown are barriers to our evolution. The origins of this fear are in part a negative view of uncertainty and change, and also a sense of risk and fear associated with a deviation from the status quo. Adapting to change is often perceived as an inefficient use of energy. As a result, we try to control our environment to eliminate uncertainty; yet in so doing, we waste energy by imposing static predictability on to the chaotic nature of life. This fear-based approach is often more energy-intensive since it is akin to swimming against the stream, instead of using and leveraging the energy of the current.

> Chaos is not order; it is a higher form of order.
> — JUDITH HOOPER AND DICK TERESI[2]

All living systems (including our own human systems, as much as we may deceive ourselves to the contrary) emerge naturally, with chaos as the overriding organizing force. Many intelligent humans have built complex computer programs to model chaos within human systems (for example, the stock market). While we have become aware of operating principles, rules, patterns and order within nature, it is chaos that is the overriding organizing force in life, eluding predictability — ordered yet spontaneous, one of life's beautiful paradoxes. Societies and economies are emergent, beyond control. Though predicting the future may be appealing, it is through understanding and aligning ourselves with the basic rules of nature that we can navigate optimal pathways for future success. Self-organization, complexity and chaos operate the ecosystems within which we live and work.

We must admire the special aspects of the human species that have allowed us to temporarily transcend some of nature's constraints and organizing forces. Yet for all the knowledge and experience of human civilization, it would be prudent also to draw upon our wisdom to respect the primacy of these organizing forces — like learning to write software in the right language. How might humans readapt to what some may view as our huge evolutionary success in habitat colonization and population growth? How might we come to terms with the notion that we are still subject to nature's laws and operate within these?

The principles of nature

Understanding the patterns and principles of nature can provide insight into how best to future-proof business for the unpredictability ahead. In the box on page 25 are some basic principles of nature according to Fritjof Capra, a renowned scientist and teacher of eco-literacy.

Biomimicry

Biomimicry is an exciting emergent discipline that explores how nature works and how we can learn from nature to solve human problems. Humans have been learning from other species for many thousands of years, yet biomimicry as a formal concept is more recent. The word "biomimicry" itself was coined by Janine Benyus (author of the book *Biomimicry*) and originates from the Greek *bios* (life) and *mimesis* (imitation). In the words of Benyus, biomimicry has three aspects to it:

Principles of nature[4]

Networks: At all scales of nature, we find living systems nesting and interconnecting within other living systems — networks within networks. Boundaries within and among systems are not boundaries of strict separation but boundaries of identity and interaction. All living systems are interconnected, communicate with one another and share resources across their boundaries.

Cycles: All living organisms must feed on continual flows of matter and energy from their environment to stay alive, and, in turn, all living organisms continually contribute flows of matter and energy to their environment. As a whole, an ecosystem generates no net waste, as one species' waste becomes another species' food with matter and energy transforming and cycling continually through the web of life.

Solar energy: Solar energy, transformed into chemical energy by the photosynthesis of green plants, is the foundation of ecological cycles (there are rare exceptional non-solar ecosystems, for example, deep sea vent ecosystems driven by energy from Earth's molten core).

Partnership: The exchange of energy and resources within an ecosystem is sustained by pervasive cooperation. Life did not take over the planet by combat but by cooperation, partnership and networking.

Diversity: Ecosystems achieve robustness and resilience through the richness and complexity of their ecological webs. The greater their biodiversity, the more resilient they will be.

Dynamic balance: An ecosystem is a flexible, responsive, ever-fluctuating network. Its flexibility is a consequence of multiple dynamic sense-and-respond feedback loops that keep the system in a state of dynamic balance. No single variable is maximized; all variables fluctuate in concert around a collective optimum.

1. Nature as model. Biomimicry is a new discipline that studies nature's models and then imitates or takes inspiration from these designs and processes to solve human problems.
2. Nature as measure. Biomimicry uses an ecological standard to judge the "rightness" of our innovations. After 3.8 billion years of evolution, nature has learned what works, what is appropriate and what lasts.
3. Nature as mentor. Biomimicry is a new way of viewing and valuing nature based not on what we can extract from the natural world, but what we can learn from it.[3]

After years of work with ecologists, Janine Benyus pulled together Nature's Laws:

Nature runs on sunlight
Nature uses only the energy it needs
Nature fits form to function
Nature recycles everything
Nature rewards cooperation
Nature banks on diversity
Nature demands local expertise
Nature curbs excesses from within
Nature taps the power of limits[5]

To provide guidance to designers using biomimicry, the Biomimicry Institute has developed a framework based on the principles and conditions under which life operates, referred to as "life's principles":

Life adapts and evolves by:
• Being locally attuned and responsive:
    • Using constant feedback loops
    • Antenna, signal, response
    • Learns and imitates
    • Resourceful and opportunistic:
        • Free energy
        • Shape rather than material

- Build from the bottom up
- Simple, common building blocks
- Running on cyclic processes
- Being resilient:
  - Decentralized and distributed
  - Redundant
  - Diverse
  - Cross-pollination, common information system (genetic)

Life creates conditions conducive to life by:
- Optimizing rather than maximizing:
  - Using multifunctional design
  - Fitting form to function
- Being interdependent:
  - Recycle all materials
  - Self-organization
- Using benign manufacturing:
  - Using life-friendly materials
  - Using water-based chemistry
  - Using self-assembly[6]

Examples of innovative biomimicry designs include the following.
- ◆ Velcro is probably one of the best-known examples of biomimicry, being invented when Swiss engineer George de Mestral in the 1940s noticed how burr hooks gripped on to fabric loops.
- ◆ More recently, the communications company Qualcomm has used the iridescent principle of butterflies and peacock feathers, which refract light to provide color. Through its product, Mirasol, it applies this refraction technique to electronic displays from cell-phones to table computers, in turn using significantly less energy while providing good usability. In 2010 they won the Best Enabling Technology award from *Laptop Magazine*.[7]
- ◆ A high-speed train front end was inspired by the kingfisher's beak, allowing more efficient travel through different air pressures (tunnel and open air). The design of the Shinkansen "bullet train" of the

West Japan Railway resulted in a quieter train and 15 percent less electricity use, even while the train travels 10 percent faster.[8]

♦ The Eastgate Building, an office complex in Harare, Zimbabwe, uses 90 percent less energy for ventilation than conventional buildings of a similar size by taking inspiration from termites' self-cooling mounds.[9]

♦ A high-performance underwater data-transmission method used in the tsunami early warning system throughout the Indian Ocean is inspired by dolphins' unique frequency-modulating acoustics, developed by a company called EvoLogics.[10]

♦ A carpet tile range for which a random design is inspired by the aesthetics of leaves on a forest floor. As a result the carpet tiles can be installed in any direction, which reduces installation time and allows replacement of single tiles without damaging the overall look of the floor. The Entropy product line became InterfaceFLOR's fastest bestseller. InterfaceFLOR estimate that the Entropy product line wastes 1.5 percent of the carpet compared with the industry average of 14 percent for broadloom carpet.[11]

♦ ReGen Energy's smart grid technology was inspired by swarms in nature (such as bee behavior), referred to as "swarm technology," in optimizing peak power loads over the network.[12]

♦ British Telecom used a biological model based on ant behavior to overhaul its phone network, avoiding a ten-year multibillion-pound exercise.[13]

As exemplified by the innovations described above, biomimicry, in the main, has been applied to product design, manufacturing, green chemistry, structural planning and architecture. However, nature's wisdom can also inspire and inform organizational transformation. Such emulation of nature's genius for organizational structures, processes and people behavior may be better described as "bio-inspired" rather than biomimetic, as it is not limited to scientific extrapolations and copying nature, but also metaphorical and behavioral inspiration, although perhaps still falling within the third part of Benyus's definition of biomimicry: "nature as mentor."

Models from nature

Let's explore some of the ways nature works and, in so doing, gain some bio-inspiration from nature's wisdom. Such inspiration can greatly help organizations in this period of volatility, a period when humanity as a global community and economy has an opportunity to positively and dramatically shift from over-exploiting nature for its own gain to understanding her innate wisdom. We can learn from her and, in so doing, work with the grain of nature, swimming with the stream of life, not against it, learning to harness the power of limits.

It is important to make clear at this juncture that in gaining inspiration from nature we do not seek to romanticize nature. Nature, like human nature, struggles for existence and includes behaviors that are "red in tooth and claw"; death that brings life is another of life's paradoxes. However, there are fundamental lessons we can learn from nature about how we can understand, live with and even leverage dynamic change and resource limitations at a product, process and system design level. We can learn how to redesign our organizations for resilience and how to live as positive participants within our ecosystems.

Let us start by exploring relationship types found in nature, as these are the interconnections and interactions where exchanges of materials, information and energy occur, and these are the basis of ecosystems.

Relationships

As in business, there are constant flows and exchanges of resources in nature: water, energy, materials, nutrients, information. Old expressions like "dog eat dog" or "the pecking order" suggest that nature's supply chains control these flows primarily via hierarchy and competition, much like conventional business models. However, competition is only one of many types of relationship that operate within the dynamic interconnected web of systems and flows that make up an ecosystem.

Relationships in nature are also multifaceted and dynamic — two organisms can have many different types of relationship over time, or even at the same time. If you look at two trees side by side in a forest, they are clearly competing for exactly the same resources in the same location, yet the trees have evolved to live together collaboratively in the forest.

Here, the benefits each organism gains from the existence of the other outweigh the costs of competition.

Different types of relationship, intended and unintended, lead to cause–consequence connections between and within the kingdoms of nature — plants, algae, animals, fungi and bacteria — allowing for coexistence benefiting and/or costing each relation. Generally, the more participants and relationships that exist in an ecosystem, the more resilient the ecosystem will be. Relationship types include predator–prey and parasitism ("win–lose," where one relation gains at the other's expense), commensalism ("win–neutral," where one gains and the other is neither directly gaining nor losing from the other) and mutualism ("win–win," where both benefit from each other). An example of a parasitic relationship is the flu bacteria in your body: the flu bacteria gain energy to live from your body, and your body loses the energy without additional benefit. An example of commensalism is the anemone fish, which gains protection living among the poisonous tentacles of the sea anemone, but offers no known benefit to its host, while causing it no harm. An example of mutualism is the relationship between bees and flowering plants, with bees gaining energy from the flowers' nectar and the plants benefiting from bee pollination.

Relationships between organisms can be also generalist or specific. In your garden, you may notice that one honeybee may pollinate many different types of flower, and that those flowers may be pollinated by a variety of different insects. These are interdependencies. Some flowers, however, can be pollinated by only one specific species of insect or bat, and perhaps only during a very few days (or nights) each year. In this case, the flower and pollinator have coevolved to perfectly meet each other's unique needs, and this is therefore a co-dependency.

In certain cases, specific partner relations are an absolute requirement for completing life cycles. Orchid seeds, for example, cannot germinate without a specific fungus, which the plants maintain in their body and pass on to the next generation of seeds. Incidentally, your body hosts more beneficial bacteria in your gut than you have human cells in your whole body; these bacteria consume and break down food in your intestine that is otherwise indigestible to you, and then release nutrients in forms that your body can use.

Nature can provide immense wisdom on which types of relationship can help you survive stress and disturbance as well as providing models and inspiration for transformation in your business. Here is an example inspired by work with Royal Botanic Gardens, Kew.[14] A relationship grouping can be demonstrated by legumes — a group of plants of mostly tropical, woody species, as well as garden peas and beans, which harbor bacteria (species of *Rhizobium*) that are specific to each legume species, in addition to fungi in their roots. While the fungi contribute to the uptake of iron and phosphorus from the soil, the bacteria capture nitrogen (gas) from the air, transforming it into a chemical form that the plants can utilize (ammonium, NH_4^+). Most interestingly, the bacteria only do this when in active partnership with legume roots — not when living alone. Nitrogen is generally a limiting nutrient in soil, yet fundamentally important to plants' growth. This important plant–fungi–bacteria relationship enables legumes to thrive in relatively poor soil and produce highly viable protein-rich seeds. This is an example of diverse multi-stakeholder collaboration for the benefit of each and all.

Parasites, pests and pathogens, on the other hand, benefit from their host by taking what they need, but without returning. Close observation reveals that virtually all such challenging organisms are limited in their choice of host — an insect pest, a fungus or a bacterium does not attack all plants or animals that it comes into contact with. Epidemics of sudden oak death, horse chestnut blight and leaf miners will reduce the availability of hosts; complete loss of the hosts will lead to loss of habitat for the pests and pathogens on which they wholly depend, leading to mutual extinction. For this reason, they often respect the host's needs and take only what is sufficient for them to live. Parasitic mistletoe can live on the same branch of a host tree for years without causing apparent damage. Trees are large enough to afford a small loss by parasitic mistletoe (or is the host gaining something from the mistletoe unknown to us?). There are few examples of pests and pathogens wiping out host plants to extinction. For example, Dutch elm disease is widespread, but so far it has failed to cause total destruction as there are still many young elms in hedgerows.

What is clear is that purely exploitative organisms can appear to be benign, but they invariably weaken the host, sometimes in a less than obvious way. Conversely, there can be organisms that at first sight appear purely exploitative, but which can have more subtle beneficial effects on their host or for the ecosystems in which they live. Such subtle benefits sometimes only become apparent in times of great strife for the host or the ecosystem.

Likewise, in business it is not always obvious which parts of the organization that are not overtly adding value are merely there for the ride, or are providing a subtle benefit unmeasured by the normal performance assessment process. Cutting dead wood from an organization in challenging times may be prudent, yet damaging a useful web of stakeholder relations in times when greater resilience is needed is not prudent. There is a fine line between prudent pruning and reducing the organization's resilience. Also, spare capacity in business, as well as nature, is important in times of transformation as it can allow for mutations and innovations to spawn. Of course, pruning without simultaneous adaptation is no better than slowing down the inevitable death — "optimizing and delaying hitting the wall." Transformative redesigning for resilience must go hand in hand with optimization — investing in the future while letting go of aspects that no longer serve the present and future purpose of the organization.

Evolutionary adaptation makes optimal use of the neighborhood and environment, adapting relationships into those that are most beneficial for the situation, for themselves and for the systems in which they operate.

According to Henry Ward, Global Supply Chain Director at Dow Chemicals:

> It's all about win–wins with you and suppliers/customers. The future is two companies coming together, defining a joint business model with both benefiting and innovating in the process.[16]

Like relationships between organisms, relationships between organizations can take many different forms, ranging from tightly coupled joint ventures to more loosely coupled preferred supplier relationships, or associates in mutually beneficial networks with diverse stakeholder communities. Within the organizational boundaries of a business there

Nature's insight — synergy and opportunity in relationships[15]

In South Africa there grows a carnivorous plant, *Roridula dentata*, which does not have the enzymes needed to digest the prey that gets trapped on its sticky leaves. The plants have formed a synergistic relationship with hemipteran insects, *Pameridea marlothi*, which consume the trapped prey. The droppings of these insects are digestible to the plant as a rich source of nitrogen. Such indirect digestion of prey accounts for up to 70 percent of the nitrogen the plant acquires. The helper hemipteran insects are not trapped by the plant as they have adapted to be able to avoid the sticky patches, so benefiting from this relationship by using the plant as a trap for otherwise difficult to catch insects sometimes much bigger than themselves. Pollination of *Roridula* is also accomplished by the *Pameridea*, so there is a tight, multifaceted, intimate one-to-one relationship. Throw the spider *Synaema marlothi* into this relationship, and we have an innocuous opportunist. It, like *Pameridea*, enjoys a meal of the trapped insect (and also, occasionally, the helpful hemipterans), but does not leave any reward in return. Although this appears to disrupt the perfectly balanced mutualism — the plant's access to nitrogen and pollination rate is reduced — the loss experienced by the plants is tolerated as part of the wider ecosystem balance. Their habitat is limited to bogs where inter-plant species competition is relatively insignificant, and so limiting population growth for this perennial, long-living plant can help ensure balance to the wider ecosystem. As with all relationships in nature, they are part of a larger system that is optimized to thrive within the natural resource limits of the local environment. As circumstances become more challenging, the relationships themselves evolve in order to adapt to changes in the environment.

can be relationships between aligned business units, communities of specialists, close-knit teams and manager–employee. In fact, without relationships, both within the organization and between organizations, none would thrive. Effective relationships between people thrive through interpersonal links founded on common values, a cooperative approach to challenges, and an attitude that you give first and receive as a result. This attitude among stakeholders emanates from a culture that is strongly bound to values of cooperation, trust and creativity, while accepting change, failure and novelty as a part of life. .

As seen in these examples from nature, relationships between and among individual organisms, as well as the organisms themselves, evolve to fit the changing landscape. Taking this inspiration from nature, we learn that creating a working environment conducive to dynamism, cooperation and creativity helps embed resilience into the business. Allowing such a working environment to flourish and evolve across the organization and business ecosystem of partners, customers and the stakeholder community becomes a predeterminate of success as the business environment becomes more volatile; it may well be a defining characteristic separating those organizations that adapt and flourish from those that perish in the times ahead.

Finding the right harmony between creativity and productivity is key, as will be fostering a sense of trust and sharing across the business ecosystem. The more we recognize the importance of resilience within organizations, the more we understand that a strong, values-led culture is a core part of redesigning for resilience.

Adnams, a small UK brewery, has been exposed to significant economic volatility over the last five years. Yet over this period it has managed to consistently outperform the market. Core to Adnams' success is its values-led culture. The relationships between teams, across the business and the business ecosystem are the lifeblood of Adnams. From the CEO to the shop floor, each person proudly upholds the values of Adnams. Such values are not watered down in times of challenge; in fact, they are what navigate the organization through uncharted waters.

In addition to the world around us, the soil beneath our feet can provide inspiration and models for organizational culture.

Inspired by soil[17]

In nature, soils are the interface between the mineral (rock) and the biological (plant) worlds, and serve as the foundation for terrestrial life. We depend on soil to grow food, process waste, filter residues, recycle nutrients and sustain the ecosystem. For many, soil appears inert; however, soil is better represented as a vibrant living body, with the sand and silt serving as the skeletal frame; the clay and humus serving as the connective tissues, tendons and muscles; and the water and dissolved solutes functioning as the lifeblood. The diverse microbial communities within soil function as the digestive and respiratory systems. The flux of nutrients, energy and life through the soil represents the soul. Although soil does not have a reproductive capacity (a key distinction of a living body), it does have the capacity to continuously regenerate, and is constantly growing, developing and evolving.

Below ground, the soil is simply bursting with life. The living community in one teaspoonful of healthy soil includes 100 million bacterial cells, hundreds of yards of fungal hyphae, 10,000 protozoans and a similar number of algal propagules, as well as larger microarthropods and worms — each playing important roles in the living ecosystem of the soil. There are primary, secondary and tertiary consumers and contributors within soil, which create a complex and multifaceted food web with a high degree of diversity, providing excellent resilience.

At ground level, soil lives in symbiosis with plant life. The plants convert solar energy to food energy that is either used within the plant or shunted into the soil as plant litter or root exudates. In the absence of this life-giving transformer of solar energy, the soil vitality would decline due to lack of energy. Likewise, the plant community could not complete life cycles without the nutrients, water and infrastructure provided by the soil ecosystem. Humans too have a synergistic relationship with soil. Almost every mineral nutrient in our bodies came from soil — our skeletons are built from calcium (Ca) and phosphorus (P) derived from soil. Most of our sustenance originates from plants that derived almost all of their nutrients and water from the soil. Our houses are built in (and sometimes from) the soil. We drive on it, walk on it, play on it, die on it and are buried in it.

Interestingly, the demise of many ancient civilizations coincides with the degradation of soil. Our present civilization's industrialized, monoculture-based agriculture and forestry demands high productivity from the soil, yet gives little back in return, depriving the soil of energy and the recycling of nutrients leading to decline in soil condition. The complex soil structure, the diverse living systems, the organic matter — the body and soul of the soil — become eroded, leaving only the skeleton. Pumping the soil with fertilizers and pesticides is like trying to maintain a human body on white bread, vitamin pills and medicine, and is therefore doomed to fail. The soil can limp along that way for a while, but productivity declines, it loses its ability to regenerate and loses its resilience ultimately collapsing. Our over-exploitative approach to soil is at direct odds with the mutuality nature's wisdom teaches us; hence, the synergistic benefits we gain from the soil are fast disappearing, leaving us with rising costs and decreasing yields — enter the food crisis now in our midst. This is a prime (and fundamental) example of the long-term damage caused as a result of our ignoring the basic tenets of nature.

In 2009, NetApp won CNN's "Best Company to Work For" award. Employee enthusiasm is based on NetApp's clear core values, a legendary egalitarian culture, and applying simple rules favoring decentralized decision-making, personal responsibility and local adaptability. For example, NetApp replaced a complicated travel policy with the simple maxim: "We are a frugal company. But don't show up dog-tired to save a few bucks. Use your common sense." Rather than writing static business plans, many NetApp units write "future histories," imagining where their business will be a year or two out.[18]

Soil is akin to organizational culture. From a rich culture, employee enthusiasm thrives. Like soil, over-exploitation through unbalanced, short-term, KPI-focused, monocultural approaches to business erode this richness that is so important to growing a resilient, vibrant business.

Now, let's take a look at fungi, which are often overlooked as uninteresting and unattractive, and yet they provide a wealth of inspiration for us.

Inspired by fungi[19]

Fungi specialize in interconnecting other living entities, with most land plants depending on them. Fungi are much older than plants. They evolved in the sea some 700 million years before plants, then moved to land 70 million years before plants. Fungi extract minerals and nutrients from rocks, which they then feed to plants in a partnership that is one of the most fundamental examples of mutualism on the planet. This partnership allowed plants to thrive on the Earth's surface, and led to the oxygenation of our atmosphere, a crucial evolutionary step for life on Earth.

While fungi gain food from the decomposition of plants, plants gain nutrients and life-supporting services from fungi. Fungi, through their underground network of mycelium fibres, connect stationary plants with hundreds of other plants, and share nutrients between plants, which encourages diversity within the ecosystem — a healthy diverse forest helps ensure the fungi live in a more resilient environment. Fungi also provide plants with protection from parasites, while also filtering out toxins that accumulate in the plants.

Mycologists Alan Rayner and Christian Taylor describe fungi as the "brains of the soil." Paul Stamets, a well-known American mycologist, eloquently states that this "neurological network of nature" senses movements of organisms across the land, taking action upon activity — like a falling branch. Fungi thrive in uncertainty, adapting to dynamic change through responsiveness, flexibility, opportunism and local attunement.

> Like a matrix, a bio-molecular superhighway, the mycelium is in constant dialogue with its environment, reacting to and governing the flow of essential nutrients cycling through the food chain.
> — Paul Stamets[20]

Fungi carry out their life's mission and ecosystem duties via four principal process types: exploration, assimilation, conservation and redistribution. A spore landing on a forest floor sends out radial networks (similar to the way our own neural networks work), which explore the surrounding forest. Then, upon finding food, they focus in, abandoning unsuccessful routes. By assimilation and effective sustainable colonization, the successful network pathway conserves and redistributes nutrients to foster ongoing viability of that part of the forest, sometimes transferring nutrients from rich areas to help poorer areas of the forest develop, thus fostering diversity and enhancing cooperation among species. This mutualism goes beyond simple win–win relationships to optimize whole-system abundance and stability, as it fosters cooperation and diversity across other species too, thus acting as the guardian and facilitator of mutualism.

> The loss of Steve Jobs caused much reflection on the reasons for his success. Many have reminded us that he did not invent the personal computer (as Edison did not invent the light bulb). What he did that was uniquely successful was to realize abundance by connecting, enhancing and leveraging existing ideas, developments, minds and markets. He was a crucial "fungus" of the digital age.

There is, of course, plenty more we can learn from the fungi kingdom both in terms of its usefulness to helping our sustainable way of life on Earth and also their inspiration with regards to organizational transformation. These networkers and facilitators of the soil are a source of wisdom in so many ways.

Many of us shy away from insects, especially when found in swarms; however, a deeper look at swarms and swarm behavior provides relevant insight for present and future business behavior.

Inspired by swarms

The idea of humans swarming is frightening, perhaps invoking visions of uncontrollable chaos or anarchy. But swarms formed by other social organisms in nature, like ants, bees and termites, are so beautifully choreographed and effective as a functioning unit that they are sometimes called "super-organisms." This leaderless collective decision-making ability is referred to as "swarm intelligence."

Eric Bonabeau and Christopher Meyer suggest that swarm behavior results in flexibility (the group can quickly adapt to a changing environment), robustness (even when one or more individuals fail, the group can still perform its tasks) and self-organization (the group needs relatively little supervision or top-down control).[21] Teamwork is self-organized and coordinated through individual insects (bottom-up emergence rather than top-down hierarchy); each insect interacts simply with the others around it. In this way, the collective can solve difficult problems that any one individual could not. It is an emergent and leaderless decision-making process based on collective support of the available options.[22]

Their foraging strategies demonstrate dynamic optimization between exploitation of existing sources and exploration for new ones. Honeybees' swarming — the splitting of the nest in two when the colony becomes too large — also suggests that organizations cannot grow forever. Once past their optimal size, they will reach a point of diminishing returns when they should spin off some of their operations.

Peter Miller, in his book *Smart Swarm*, identifies principles behind swarm behavior, such as indirect collaboration, self-organization and diversity of information. "Stigmergy" is a term used to describe indirect collaboration enabled through environmental modifications (e.g., ants laying down pheromone trails). The Internet is a good example of "stigmergy"; users modify their virtual environment through communication with each other. For example, a wiki could be compared to how a termites' mound is formed, one user leaving a seed of an idea, which another adds to, and so on, leading to an elaborate structure of connected thoughts.[23]

Swarms are another example of nature's chaos–order paradox, which we touched on earlier. If you watch a collection of ants for a while, the movement of any given ant appears to be chaotic or random. Each ant, however, behaves according to a set of simple rules underlying its apparent chaotic movement to give order. Watching the ants together in their hill, one would again assume there is utter chaos, but again we find there is great order within the collective whole. The lesson is that order — in the form of a clear vision, common values, a few simple rules and collective commitment to well-defined positive outcomes — allows freedom of creative personal choice in how a job might be accomplished. Collectively, this seemingly chaotic diversity and creativity flourishing through bottom-up emergence can yield far more responsive, self-adapting organizational behavior than top-down command-and-control approaches, and with much less costly management.

This insight from nature supports a virtuous cycle approach to organizational learning and culture. The more that individuals in an organization are allowed the freedom to behave and work in ways that uniquely optimize their skills and choices, the more they can support the underlying order, as well as the goals of the organization as a whole. So the idea is not to completely let go and allow chaos to reign — the idea is to create a foundation and framework (order) based on clear vision and values that support, foster and empower individual creativity and productivity (chaos), which in turn results in a high-performing cohesive collaborative collective (order).

In this framework, leaders do not dictate or control, but rather constantly share and reinforce the vision and values of the organization by clearly communicating the characteristics of positive outcomes and empowering the individuals to go about their tasks in the best way they know. Bottom-up, emergent, values-led organizational governance enables greater local attunement for individuals to adapt and respond to local issues as they arise.

Feedback

An important element of local attunement and empowerment is effective feedback. Feedback consists of the signals and responses an organism exchanges with its environment. In nature, no living system can survive long without feedback, and so we see that feedback is a necessary condition for both individual and system survival. In fact, the ability to respond to feedback in the most optimal way helps drive the success of that organism; its effectiveness at responding to feedback being what drives its positive adaptation to environment changes.

Nature is interconnected and interdependent, with every part of the ecosystem functioning as part of myriad seamless endless cycles. These beautifully coordinated cycles of nutrients, energy, water, materials and information are possible because of the feedback loops. Feedback loops are nature's way of "staying in sync" with ever-changing conditions.

Complete feedback loops are composed of three parts: the information, the receiver and the response. Each of these elements must be present and effective for the feedback loop to do its job. The information must be receivable and received by the intended recipient, and the information must trigger the appropriate response. In nature, feedback loops are embedded at all scales in time and space — immediate to very long-term, micro to macro. The presence of these sense-and-respond feedback loops means that collections of different species can live together in a highly coordinated and effective manner, without the need for overarching decision-making. They allow each participant in the system to contribute to the system while looking out for itself. Nature's feedback loops are open-source, yet are focused and targeted to achieve the desired responses while avoiding information overload. Filtering out background noise irrelevant to the job in hand is an important part of tuning in.

Virgin has created more than 300 branded companies worldwide, operating in diverse business sectors, most notably travel, media, leisure and finance. It employs approximately 50,000 people in 30 countries, with revenues exceeding £11.5 billion in 2009. Virgin operates as a structure of loosely linked autonomous units run by self-managed teams that share a brand name and values. It believes in the "power of entrepreneurship and innovation to help us rise to the new challenges that we all face." Units make their own business decisions appropriate for their market conditions; they have the benefit of autonomy coupled with the benefit — where and when it is needed — of scale and cross-fertilization. Like a swarm in nature, what appears to be chaos is not. "Contrary to what some people may think, our constantly expanding and eclectic empire is neither random nor reckless. Each successive venture demonstrates our devotion to picking the right market and the right opportunity."[24]

Swarms and other tight-knit groups of organisms (like schools of fish) function without a leader because of highly effective feedback loops. If you walked into a bat cave, you'd be overwhelmed by a confusing cacophony of screeches (not to mention the smell); however, each mother–baby bat pair has a uniquely tuned feedback loop, so that each mother can quickly and easily find her own baby among the noisy crowd. Feedback loops occur between different species too, sometimes via a cascade of information exchanges and responses.

Within the organization, well-designed feedback loops at all levels enable highly targeted and locally attuned responses to occur in sync with information received and processed locally. This can dramatically reduce management, delays and mismatched or ineffective responses. Effective feedback happens through the empowerment of employees to make appropriate decisions and take appropriate and effective real-time actions that are aligned with the vision and values of the business, avoiding the need to go through a series of vertical decision-making channels. As in nature, this is not a chaotic free-for-all; effective feedback loops need to be thoughtfully designed and fit for purpose, recognizing and matching information, receiver and response to optimize desired results. Effective feedback loops allow an organization to let go of conventional top-down organizational decision-making structures and become more responsive, adaptive, locally attuned, optimized and effective — continually fit for purpose in a changing context. Again, layers of costly management can be redirected to more value-enhancing activity.

It can sometimes be a challenge for individuals and organizations to value feedback that may be critical, even though this brings great benefit for positive improvement. Encouraging a trusting environment in which people can be open and responsive to feedback is therefore a key component of positive adaptation.

Many of us have trouble envisioning functioning as part of a leaderless swarm or playing different roles within dynamic systems, particularly in a business setting. Upon reflection, however, we find that we can quite effectively maintain multiple relationships and undertake multiple roles in several systems simultaneously, without a single leader telling us what to do. In fact, the goal is allowing these multiple roles and

In December 1999, Doug Daft took over as CEO of Coca-Cola and was charged with turning round the century-old, conservative and hierarchically structured organization. To transform it into "something nimble, agile, creative, responsive and dynamic," he said, "we had to be responsive to local markets. We had to learn." This transformation came less from top-down control, more from bottom-up empowerment and local attunement, which encouraged high-performing, locally focused, diverse teams to flourish. "The more diverse the people in a business, the greater its capacity to respond to any change in the market-place," said Daft.[25]

In early 2008, before the global recession, Tata predicted there would be an imbalance in the soda-ash market following the Beijing Olympics, and created a program within its chemical division called ADAPT (Action plan for Downturn Alleviation and Profiting in Turbulence). When the global financial crisis started, the program's scope was extended across all divisions within the group (over 90 companies). Tata empowered its employees by integrating them fully into the ADAPT program. Apart from the intended improvement in profitability, Tata benefits from a strong workforce who have gained experience in facing bad times and who have learned through seeking out positive adaptation in challenging market circumstance.

Semco, a Brazil-based multibillion-dollar company with over 3,000 workers, is often called one of the most interesting companies in the world. There are no job titles, no written policies, no HR department, nor even a headquarters at the time of writing. There is a CEO, but half a dozen senior executives pass the title every six months. All other employees are associates. People set their own salaries and working hours. Everybody shares in the profits. Everyone in the company knows what everyone else does. Every employee receives the company's financial statements and can take classes on how to read them. Team members choose their managers by vote and evaluate them, with the results being posted publicly. Meetings are voluntary, and two seats at board are open to the first employees who turn up.[26]

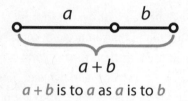

$a + b$ is to a as a is to b

Figure 4. The golden section.

experiences to mutually benefit each other as the values and behaviors become congruent. In the business world, we historically feel the need to cling to a singular title, role and rigid pattern of interactions and hier-archies, even though we know they constrain us from realizing our full potential. Different roles do not need to compete for attention; they can feed off each other's creative energy, providing synergy and abundance, not scarcity and stress.

Harnessing the power of limits

There are proportions and patterns running through nature and the wider universe. It is as if there is a "grammar of harmony" (to use HRH The Prince of Wales's words[27]) running through all of life, which we would do well to become conscious of. The golden section (also re-ferred to as the golden ratio) is one such reciprocal relationship we find throughout nature. The golden section is where the smaller part stands in the same proportion to the large part as the large part stands to the whole.

The reciprocity of this relationship is found in music, architecture, flowers, our bones, credit card design, you name it. Where it exists, it provides something naturally pleasing to the human senses—a har-mony. The harmonics in music derive from this same reciprocal rela-tionship. This is also where the Fibonacci series originates and the golden ratio (also known as the golden mean and golden number phi, or roughly 1.618). It frequents organic growth, as if the emergence within life itself follows a harmony. What is sometimes overlooked in seeing these harmonious patterns is that there is a union of complementary but differing rhythms within these harmonious patterns; for example, the relationship between the major and minor scales in music, the relationship of the sun and moon, yin and yang, and so on. Harmonies arise through the uniting of differing parts of the whole creating other stages in the relationship while still maintaining the integrity of the parts that make up the relationship.

This union of differing relationships is vital to life — an opposing yet synergistic energy that drives organic growth. This is what György Doczi refers to as *dinergy* (his own word created by combining the Greek *dia* [through] and energy), rather than synergy; synergy refers to the joining of cooperative forces, whereas it is the joining of differing tensions that creates this dinergy.[28] This goes directly to the root of one of life's perplexing paradoxes exploring why we need a yin and a yang duality in life. The creative union between these seemingly opposing forces is what drives organic growth and breathes life. It is these dinergic harmonies that naturally please us in nature — whether it be looking at a leaf or listening to musical melodies.

> If we look closely at a flower, and likewise at other natural and man-made creations, we find a unity and an order common to all of them. This order can be seen in certain proportions which appear again and again, and also in the similarly dynamic way all things grow or are made — by union of complementary opposites.
> — GYÖRGY DOCZI[29]

As we explore in Module Five, quantum theory helps explain to us how wave patterns permeate life: light, sound, magnetism, and so on. We can best see (or imagine) these wave fields when we drop a stone into a still pond. Drop a second stone in and you can watch the constructive (waves combining in phase) and destructive (waves combining out of phase) interference as waves interact. This is analogous with what emanates around us all the time in nature and business. We are all transmitters and receivers of wave fields through our senses and also our own energy fields, which we emit but cannot see. We can share the same vibration rates as others and also different vibration rates, as we each fluctuate with our environment and intent. It is the sharing of diversities of these wave patterns that gives life its immense beauty and vibrant variety. Through sharing relationships (interacting vibrations) life creates diversity, which breeds and supports more life. This is the paradox of reciprocal relationships — in sharing one's limitations with another, we complement each other, in turn providing harmony in life. This is what Doczi refers to as "the power of limits," where limitations interact to provide openness beyond those inherent limitations. This is how life grows, how it interacts with seemingly opposing forces to create new growth which can then interact with other oncoming limiting forces or factors. The power of limits is what drives creativity in life — it is "the force behind creation." As Hunter Lovins put it, "Nature uses limits as the crucible within which it creates";[30] and, in the words of HRH the Prince of Wales, "The closer we dance to the rhythms and patterns that lie within us, the closer we get to acting in what is the right way."[31]

If you are interested in the power of limits and the harmony of life, then I strongly recommend you read both *The Power of Limits* by György Doczi and *Harmony* by HRH The Prince of Wales, Tony Juniper and Ian Skelly, which provide more comprehensive coverage of this fascinating and yet complex area.

Industrial ecology

Industrial ecology (and within it, industrial symbiosis) is a growing discipline that applies nature's operating principles to industry.[32] An important and fundamental aspect of industrial ecology is enabling waste of one process to be food of another, hence generating benefit rather than cost. While industrial ecology has traditionally focused on the product and process aspects of the organization, the same principles can apply to people behavior and stakeholder relationships. Just as an organism fills a niche within its ecosystem and food web, so does an organization fill a niche within its business ecosystem (the stakeholder community across the social, economic and environmental landscapes within which the organization operates). Waste becoming food for another process or partner has more recently been referred to as the "closed loop model" or "circular economy."

The closed loop model is a biomimetic approach, a school of thought that takes nature as an example and considers that our systems should work like organisms, processing nutrients that can be fed back into the cycle — hence the "closed loop" or "regenerative" terms usually associated with it.

— ELLEN MACARTHUR FOUNDATION[33]

Industrial ecology challenges the over-exploitative nature of the current "take–make–waste" industrial paradigm. It uses inspiration from nature in exploring how systems can be more interconnected and less linear — where waste of one part of the ecosystem is input for another, and hence there is no need for wasteful emissions of any kind (whether gas, liquid or solid waste), as long as the right interconnections are in place. Today there are many organizations embracing the core principles of industrial ecology while seeking to "reach zero" in their waste emissions. Unilever, Johnson & Johnson, Nike, AT&T, Novo Nordisk, InterfaceFLOR and Dow Chemicals are just some of the better-known brands among a growing group of manufacturers exploring industrial ecology. Such focus on reaching zero-emissions brings win–wins (and often synergistic multiple wins) of reduced long-term costs as well as improved value creation through innovation and collaboration across the business ecosystem.

In order for organizations to radically reduce waste emissions and other negative impacts, they need to radically rethink and redesign their products and production lines, from upstream design and input sourcing to downstream product-use behaviors and end-of-life disposal. Such redesigning of product material flows is greatly facilitated by the collective intelligence that emerges from collaboration within the business ecosystem, across organizational boundaries and among traditionally siloed departments within the organization.

This is a positive evolution in the paradigm of manufacturing (which is still characterized by a "culture of monoculture" focused primarily on economies of scale and product homogeneity), adapting it to that which is more in harmony with nature, where waste is food and where economies of scope balance economies of scale.

"Cradle to cradle" is an important approach brought to life by William McDonough and Michael Braungart in their book of the same name. In this approach, material and technological flows in industry imitate nature's "waste = food" system of nutrient flows, where form follows evolution not just function:

> The "right things" for manufacturers and industrialists to do are those that lead to "good growth" — more niches, health, nourishment, diversity, intelligence and abundance — for this generation of inhabitants on the planet and for generations to come.[34]

Similarly, in the words of Janine Benyus:

> As the Japanese industrial ecologist Michiyuki Uenohara says, we have plenty of "arteries" — ways for products to flow from the heart of manufacturers into the body of the economy — but we need "veins" as well, ways to return the products so that their materials can be purified and reused. The more veins and arteries you add to a system, the more complex it becomes, and the more cooperation you need for proper functioning.[35]

In nature, materials flow easily within and around an ecosystem, usually passing through the soil along the way. Recycling in nature is not "closed loop," in the sense that an apple is not recycled back into an apple. An apple, or the materials that once made up an apple, may become part of a bird, or a worm, or soil humus, or your body, or that of a horse or a plant. Animals, plants, algae, fungi and bacteria are all very different, yet they (and we) are all made of the same handful of basic elemental building blocks (mostly carbon, nitrogen, oxygen, hydrogen, phosphate, calcium and sulphur). The fact that we all have interchangeable parts enables the materials of life to flow through myriad diverse decomposition and utilization pathways in endless everlasting cycles: resilient recycling.

What does this suggest? If we made all of our outputs from the same small set of molecules that life is made of, and if we manipulated them using water-based chemistry and solar energy, our industries could be in harmony with nature.

What else does this tell us? Do we need to adhere to the "sacrifice" model of sustainability (i.e., to give up things we like in order to be sustainable)? Growth and consumption need to fit the system context and the ecosystem's carrying capacity. For example, in countries such as Bangladesh people are consuming water in time-honored ways — ways that were once sustainable and in harmony with the local ecosystems. The problem is that this type of water use is no longer sustainable, as a result of population growth. The cumulative actions of individuals are leading to systemic problems (i.e., groundwater depletion). On the other hand, do we need to consume less and restrict economic growth if our consumption and growth are in harmony with our ecosystem (social, environmental and economic ecosystem)? For example, gardeners hope their resident worms are copious consumers, thus enriching the soil. They also hope their plants will grow through indulging in all the sunlight, water and nutrients they need, thus providing us with food, the waste of which is composted, again enriching the soil and feeding the cycle.

The sacrifice model of sustainability sometimes suggests growth is bad. Certainly, growth in acres of paved surfaces and piles of toxic waste is bad, but growth in nature — growth that is in harmony with the ecosystem — is not only good, it is beautiful. And we know that growth in some aspects of human nature — love, creativity, wisdom — is not only good and beautiful, it also begets more of the same in a virtuous cycle.

How can we tell the difference between good growth and bad growth? We have already explored the importance of feedback loops in nature. There are many different kinds of feedback loop, but let's consider two basic types: negative feedback loops and positive feedback loops. A negative feedback loop is where the results of an action or activity tend to reduce that action or activity. For example, the more you eat, the less you want to eat. It is how nature keeps itself in check when too much of a good thing is a bad thing. A positive feedback loop is when the results of an action or activity drive more of the same activity. In spite of the name, positive feedback loops are not always positive: greed tends to beget more greed; power tends to beget more power; the purchase of one new item can fuel the desire to purchase more new

Marks & Spencer, as part of their Plan A initiative, have launched the UK's first closed-loop recycling plant, which turns waste packaging into new packaging. The initiative not only helps reduce waste, but educates and engages with local communities and potential customers in a positive way, encouraging people to be part of a solution.

Denmark's Kalundborg ecopark exemplifies industrial ecology, with interdependence between organizations, the local community and environment through shared relationships and resources, where waste of one becomes food for the other. At the center is the Asnæs Power Station, a 1,500MW coal-fired power plant, which has material and energy links with the community and several other companies. Surplus heat from this power plant is used to heat 3,500 local homes, in addition to a nearby fish farm, whose sludge is then sold as a fertilizer. Steam from the power plant is sold to Novo Nordisk, a pharmaceutical and enzyme manufacturer, in addition to a Statoil plant. This reuse of heat reduces the amount of thermal pollution discharged into a nearby fjord. Additionally, a by-product from the power plant's sulphur dioxide scrubber contains gypsum, which is sold to a wallboard manufacturer. Almost all of the manufacturer's gypsum needs are met this way, which reduces the amount of open-pit mining needed. Furthermore, fly ash and clinker from the power plant are used for road building and cement production.[36]

The demand for caviar has resulted in a significant decline in sturgeon populations. Fish farming is a viable solution, but it generates its own environmental problems. Following the concepts of industrial ecology, Andrew Barker Lepton Employment (ABLE) set up the From Cardboard to Caviar project. Here's how it works: waste cardboard generated by stores and restaurants is shredded and used as horse bedding. The soiled bedding material is composted by worms in a process called vermi-composting. The reproducing worms are fed to sturgeon fish, which produce caviar. The caviar is sold back to the restaurants and stores that generate the waste cardboard. Not only is this an example of industrial ecology, it's also an example of how consumption and growth in harmony with nature can be a good thing.[37]

items. To assess when growth is good or bad, reflect on the type of feed-back loop that it creates. If growth creates well-being, then more of that growth and well-being can be good. If growth inflicts social and environmental harm, then more of that growth and harm is not good.

Emergence

The concept of emergence, and emergent processes and behavior, is fundamental to how nature operates. Fritjof Capra noted that "throughout the living world, the creativity of life expresses itself through the process of emergence."[38] We all know the feeling when one plus one is greater than two; when the whole is greater than the sum of the parts; when a single conversation can be life-changing. As children, we were delighted to see a recognizable image appear when we simply drew an ordered sequence of lines in a dot-to-dot drawing. And no matter how much gardening we do, it is always magical to watch sprouts pop up out of the soil a few days after we plant them.

All biological systems have an emergent quality, as all living structures (including social and organizational) are emergent structures. Emergence has a self-generating quality, where individual parts of an ecosystem interact to provide an emergent order (an unfolding of events that are self-fuelled by the actions and interactions of the parts). Emergence is when an organized, complex and/or cohesive pattern or result arises — often unpredictably — from a series of individually simple component interactions. This is the nature of nature. Emergent systems exhibit synergistic effects, where the individual parts (aware or not) interrelate and, in so doing, provide synergies, where the interaction of the whole is greater than the sum of its parts involved in the interaction. This synergy is what feeds the growth of the ecosystem and provides for its emergent behavior. Humans are part of biotic life, and we too exhibit emergent behavior (from stock-market trends to World Wide Web interactivity). It is as if the collective whole, through the interaction of the parts, self-organizes as a whole. Hence the notions of relationships, communities, ecosystems and Gaia itself all being part of an emergent interrelated community of parts.

Emergence in human behavior is linked to decentralized, distributed decision making and self-learning, which requires a degree of openness and self-criticism. Critical self-reflection requires stepping out of one's comfort zone, which is not easy at the organizational or personal level. Emergence in business therefore requires a higher level of intellectual and emotional maturity, moral integrity and courage than is currently found in the prevailing business ethos of today. It is also important to point out that the level of emergence may vary depending on the organization's challenges, and may also vary by area (team, department, focus group) within the organization.

Conventional thinking suggests that if you want to accomplish something, particularly something complex, you need to fully articulate the desired result, analyze the situation, create a step-by-step plan, gather needed resources and then execute the plan to completion. If all works well, you will end up with the desired or predicted result. While operating in volatile, dynamically changing environments, there is also a need for innovative and radical redesign, to drive toward as-yet-unimagined results, to accomplish things that have never been done before. How do you accomplish results you cannot even describe? How do you tick boxes that don't yet exist? Like nurturing seedlings in fertile soil, if you put the right resources together under the right conditions, emergence just happens. It is what happens naturally when all players understand their context, and the speed, scale and scope of what is needed, being empowered to execute the collective vision through individual interactions and emergent behavior.

The concepts of emergence, emergent behavior and emergent processes are core to chaos theory and systems thinking. Emergence is how complexity and diversity are created from simplicity, and how the apparently chaotic behavior of swarms can result in self-organizing super-

We are participating in the largest value-generating emergent process in human history, made possible by the Internet and mobile communication technologies. Individually and collectively, we have all gained incredible value from our use of and participation in "the cloud," which in turn has led to the emergence of new value. No single overarching governor owns, controls, manages or directs—it is entirely emergent.

organisms. The collection of the parts — interconnected within a network of synergistic relationships, all contributing to the system while functioning independently — forms a dynamic resilient whole, the properties of which cannot be predicted by analyzing the parts.

Collective adaptation emerges from the collective whole as individual members strive to adapt and enhance themselves and their relationships to generate more benefits for themselves and the whole. Order in the chaos of emergence comes through shared values, the core behavioral patterns that provide cohesion and common goal.

In summary, successful emergence at an organizational level requires deeply understanding what "good" looks like, "letting go" of predictability and stepping out of comfort zones, being okay with ambiguity, working with dynamic tension, being flexible and patient, and operating at a higher level of trust and intellectual and moral maturity than is typically found in a firm of the past.

Organisms and super-organisms

In certain collective groupings of organism behavior, the notion of the "super-organism" has been explored. An organism (as defined in the dictionary) is a form of life composed of mutually dependent parts that maintain various vital processes. The notion of the super-organism refers to a collective of single organisms that mutually depend on each other while maintaining vital parts of the overall community — for example, an ant colony has been referred to as a super-organism. Group adaptation can influence individual adaptation and vice versa, giving rise to emergence within organizations, communities (and societies). Yet this does not presuppose (or for that matter restrict) the evolution toward a super-organism. Hence, an organization (as a collective of people synergistically processing for the collective whole) can exhibit emergent behavior like other biological systems, and can be viewed as a living, emergent organism (with or without necessarily being defined as a "super-organism"). We do not need to be bogged down by definitions of organism and super-organism; it is sufficient to say that an organization can be described and referred to as a living organism in a practical sense, even if not in a strict scientific sense.

Ecological dynamics

Our explorations so far have revealed that organisms, organizations and systems in life are dynamic and responsive — changes are occurring at all levels and at all times. In addition to this state of "dynamic non-equilibrium," ecosystems themselves adapt and evolve over periods of time in a process referred to as ecological succession.

At school many of us may have been taught ecological succession as a series of one-way stages; for example, the stages a piece of land undergoes on its way from bare ground to mature ecosystem. Without further explanation, one would assume that upon reaching maturity the ecosystem stayed essentially the same until some natural disaster damaged it or wiped it out completely. Although this succession to maturity does indeed occur, the process is more complex and — you guessed it — more dynamic than previously understood. Ecosystems themselves undergo dynamic succession.

Scientific research into ecological dynamics has identified different stages of development that occur within an ecosystem, and how ecosystems as a whole develop and cycle through stages. This is best described through the "adaptive cycle," which has been defined and explored in terms of natural and human systems in the book *Panarchy* by Lance H. Gunderson and C. S. Holling, along with the work of the Resilience Alliance.[39]

Four distinct phases have been identified:
1. growth (r)
2. conservation (K)
3. collapse or release (Ω)
4. reorganization (α).

The adaptive cycle exhibits two major phases (or transitions). The first (often referred to as the front loop or foreloop), from r to K, is the slow, incremental phase of growth and accumulation. The second (referred to as the back loop), from omega to alpha, is the rapid phase of reorganization leading to renewal. During the slow front phase of the cycle, connectedness and stability increase. The back loop represents a rapid phase of release and reorganization, which leads once again to a time of growth.[40]

As noted earlier, we tend to view development of an organization or an ecosystem as growing from a pioneering, immature stage to a mature stage, and then staying in the mature phase in more or less a steady state. We tend to imagine a bare stretch of land transforming over time from fast-growing, opportunistic, pioneering weeds to grass, then to scrubland and then to mature forest. Similarly in business, we can imagine the transformation from start-up to small-to-medium-sized enterprise and then to market leader. Once there, we feel we ought to hold tightly to a position of dominance. Yet this one-way growth model misses out the important decline and collapse stage (which is often ignored or not talked about in human systems as it is seen negatively by dominant social view). The collapse stage is the important back loop that connects the cycle from growth and steady state to decline, collapse and regrowth. In life, it would seem, in order to have a breakthrough we need a breakdown, just as day comes with night, a party with a hangover and life with death. It is this reciprocal relationship of yin and yang again, playing out in a dynamic evolutionary way, something we cannot escape from in life and would do well to work with rather than fight against.

Dynamic succession stages in natural and human systems are present within life at all levels — microbiology, ecosystems and human societies. This is the time dynamic, within which matter and life, and the

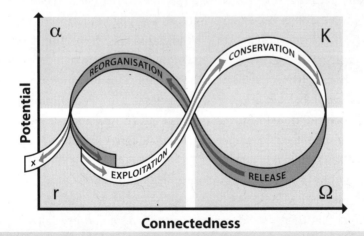

Figure 5. The adaptive cycle.
Reproduced with permission from Gunderson, L. and Holling, C. (2002). *Panarchy: Understanding Transformations in Human and Natural Systems*. Washington, DC: Island Press, p.34.

The adaptive cycle[41]

The first phase of growth we call the "front loop," and it represents a process of increasing efficiency and a learning process that occurs in small steps; it is incremental. That is when efficiencies in production of a product or sequestering of biomass are controlled by a smaller number of dominant elements or species. The second phase we call the "back loop," and it represents the freeing or collapse of earlier control, the expansion of resilience and a learning process that occurs as a bigger jump.... Panarchy adds the idea of a hierarchy of adaptive cycles working in two ways, between small and fast cycles and big and slow cycles. This two-way interaction between cycles of the panarchy represents the way living systems both persist (from memory of the large and slow) and yet innovate (from revolt of the small and fast). It shows how small and big and fast and slow events and processes can transform ecosystems and organisms through evolution, or can transform humans and their societies through learning, or the chance for learning.

---

relations between matter and living beings, oscillate — the "wave of life." The beautiful complexity of life is that this wave of continual adaptation takes place simultaneously at all scales of life systems, all having differing rates and paces of growth and regrowth, and hence differing harmonics of this wave of life. Becoming aware of, aligning with and learning to leverage the harmonics that your organization is both emitting and subject to will greatly help your understanding of dynamic transformation, and so help light up the path for successful transformative evolution with its inevitable, yet unpredictable cycles of growth and transformation. Successful transformation is less about control and predictability and more about flexible recombinations of adaptive interdependent systems within systems.

Sometimes these recombinations grow and then stabilize, and at other times they help open windows of instability, leading to new combinations that then provide new growth. Failure and breakdown can thereby be as instructive as success and breakthrough. This dynamic non-equilibrium in business requires a shift in conventional management thinking from over-reliance on top-down, hierarchical approaches to managing within complexity. Managing within complexity juggles and combines varying styles and techniques.[42] It encourages bottom-up emergence to flourish, guided by an all-pervasive values-led work ethic. We explore this further in Modules Three, Four and Five.

Small, medium or large systems of all shapes and sizes dynamically adapt in the same way. For example, cycles within an economy — boom to bust to boom again. Also, cycles at a product level: a new product release following a new, innovative breakthrough, leading to growth in market share, followed by a period of slower growth, eventual stagnation and decline in market share, then to product expiration and new innovation. The same is true, of course, for the birth, youth, maturity, old age and death of each of us. We also find a cycle within the day, lunar month, season and year. At a larger timescale, the cycle of human civilization experiences the stages of the adaptive cycle. On a macro-scale, we find the same cycle on Earth with the mass explosions of biodiversity, mass extinctions and stages in between. At an even larger scale, we are beginning to realize that galaxies too follow this dynamic of expansion, steady state and then contraction to collapse and rebirth again.

In becoming aware of the ever-present cycles of life within everything, inward and outward, we learn to recognize the breakdowns and breakthroughs as positive stages within our evolution. Our organizations ought not to expend vital energy trying to control their environments, trying to resist any part of the adaptive cycle other than growth. This is resisting evolution, and it is a futile waste of energy, while also slowing down effective transformation for the organization within its dynamic business environment. Of far greater use is awareness and understanding of the dynamic environment one is operating in and the ability to adapt to it. Some parts of the organization may be at the rapid growth stage, while others may simultaneously be declining and heading for rebirth.

The greater the diversity of stages the organization can exhibit within itself (by fostering creativity and diversity) and within its wider business ecosystem (through partnerships and alliances), the greater the resilience of the organization, and hence the more success the organization has in transforming and evolving, and so continuing to generate value for its stakeholder community. Decline can be just as useful as growth. The collapse of one part of an organization can lead to the release of new innovations (the breakdown leading to a breakthrough): failure viewed as a learning that yields success. Business models and business ecosystems that encourage interrelated parts to grow and collapse in line with their own harmonics gain greater strategic resilience. As we saw in the example earlier, the Virgin Group is made up of distinct businesses, all

Nokia is one of the most recognized mobile-phone brands in the world. Its success and sustainability are based on embracing the concept of succession: "Over the past 150 years, Nokia has evolved from a riverside paper-mill in southwestern Finland to a global telecommunications leader connecting over 1.3 billion people. During that time, we've made rubber boots and car tires. We've generated electricity. We've even manufactured TVs. Changing with the times, disrupting the status quo—it's what we've always done. And we fully intend to keep doing it."[44] In fact, the current challenges Nokia faces have been put down to its not adapting fast enough in recent years.

Nike has experienced periods of rapid growth, interrupted with periods of flat or declining growth. It has lived and breathed the ecological succession stages, and survived to tell the tale. The key to Nike's continued success has been its ability to learn and adapt as an organization. In the early 1980s it moved from growth phase to conservation, then decline and reorganization. By the end of the early 1990s, Nike had reorganized into a decentralized, diverse, differentiated business. During the 1990s it again experienced succession through growth (sales rose from US$2 billion to US$9 billion) to decline, being hit by an external shock of exposure through Internet activism about child labor in its factories. Nike positively adapted by admitting to the problem and radically improving ethical standards and approaches across its operations and supply chain. Adapting to feedback from its business environment has enabled Nike to be successful in weathering storms along its journey.

at different stages of growth, all with their own business ecosystems, yet all interconnected through a common brand and business ethic.

Organizational success is about moving forward, not simply excelling in a static position. Indeed, overcoming disturbances provides the imperative to adapt and learn. It is the overcoming of disturbances that brings success. In the words of Tachi Kiuchi and Bill Shireman, "To "succeed" literally means to follow in order; to move from one phase to the next."[43] Hence, optimal business behavior in our volatile times becomes less about solving problems and more about working toward positive outcomes; less about trying to redirect the stream of life and more about learning to swim with the stream, to ride the waves and use the undercurrents, and to tune in to the harmonic of life and find your organization's sweet melody.

In summary, all living systems are dynamic and operate in dynamic non-equilibrium, which means they constantly change and adapt, going through phases of growing, collapsing, reorganizing and regrowing within the context of the wider environment which is also continuously changing. Nothing is static, everything is dynamic. Nothing is isolated or separate, everything is interconnected.

Shamanic business[45]

Shamanism is about deep empathy with the world around us, living in right relationships with all beings, and sensing and responding to our living, emergent environment. As a species, it would seem that humans have been around for about 200,000 years. Until we discovered agriculture about 11,000 years ago, all humans were hunter-gatherers, as far as we know. In order to survive and thrive, humans learned how to connect with everything around them, viewing and sensing the interconnected web of life. Back then, we all had a deep empathy with our environment.

This deep empathy is the essence of what shamanism is. Shamanism is not a religion. Rather, it is our natural state of being. For the vast majority of human history, it was how we related to, and experienced, the world. All hunter-gatherer tribes (and so all of our ancestors for literally tens of thousands of years) lived shamanically. In his book *The Fall*, Steve Taylor shows that, far from living brutish lives, hunter-gatherers tended to live peacefully, with excellent mental health, functioning co-operatively, efficiently and, above all, sustainably.[46]

Over the years, as we became more mechanized and materially fo-cused, we started to lose our empathic bonds with nature, thereby losing our connection with our environment. Along with this disconnection, this "fall," we have lost our ability to live in harmony with nature, and in turn with ourselves, leading us to increased propensity for dis-ease and stress. Shamanic cultures tend to take only what they need and leave the rest to thrive in nature, hence preventing over-exploitation of the envi-ronment. Our prevalent way is of taking more than we need, and more than is sustainable; hence the over-exploitation of our environment that we witness today. When we lost shamanism, we lost our way; we lost our empathy and connectedness. Business would do well to embrace the core concepts of shamanism, to help healthy practices and right rela-tions to grow and flourish.

Shamanic business is business that works in "right relationship" (harmony) with its people and resources, and is engaged in "right ac-tion" (values-led and sustainable). It is business behavior that is deeply rooted in ethics and sustainability. Shamanic business is authentic busi-ness, lasting business and good business sense.

In studying different shamanic cultures, the anthropologist Michael Harner realized that there was a remarkable consistency of thought, be-liefs and practices between shamanic cultures worldwide. He coined the phrase "core shamanism" for these common practices.[47] Our tribal an-cestors used to take the core shamanic practices and adapt them to the times and environment in which they lived. The shamanic practices in-stilled a deep sense of empathy and reverence for all life; empathy with other human beings, other animals, other plants and the environment as a whole. Shamanic principles and practices were central to the tribe living in a functional, cooperative and sustainable way.

Harner took these core shamanic practices and adapted them (just as our ancestors have always done), distilling them into a form that is applicable to modern Western industrial culture. Core shamanism pro-vides us with an easily learned set of practices that can help us reconnect to that profound sense of reverence for all life that our ancestors had. It

Innocent (parent company Fresh Trading Ltd) produce fruit smoothies, juice and "veg pot" products, sold in supermarkets and grocery stores. In its first five years, Innocent revenues grew from £6 million in 2002 to £114 million in 2007. In 2010 Innocent had 250 employees in the UK, 36 different products, market share of 77.5 percent and products in 10,000 retailers. It is now the number one smoothie brand in Europe. Key to Innocent's success is the ethical and healthy character of the business. It has one core principle from which all decisions flow: "Create a business we can be proud of." This includes actively looking after the health and well-being of their consumers, their employees, their communities and their ecosystems.[48]

can help regain our sense of deep empathy that we have lost, and which we desperately need back. Here are some basic principles of core shamanism:

1. Everything is made of energy (spirit).
2. This energy/spirit is alive and conscious.
3. Everything is therefore alive and conscious.
4. Everything is part of a living, interconnected web of energy, which we humans are part of.
5. Everything is conscious and interconnected, and so everything can be "communicated" with (this can be done through what is known as "shamanic journeying," and can also be done through awareness and intention).
6. When we communicate with things, we understand them and feel empathy with them.
7. Thus, shamanic practices bring a deep, heartfelt empathy with, and reverence for, all things.
8. This helps us live in harmony and "right relationship" with each other as people and the environment, and engage in "right action."
9. Human beings have the (seemingly unique) ability to "unplug" themselves from the web.
10. This unplugs us from this sense of empathy and "right relationship," and we no longer act with "right action."

11. This makes us ill individually, as organizations and as societies (physically, mentally, emotionally and spiritually), and leads to us harming others and the environment, and acting in unsustainable ways.

12. In unplugging and separating off we lose something profound. This is known as "soul loss" (or "power loss").[49]

13. Healthy human beings (and so, healthy human organizations and societies) feel part of nature, not separate from it; not above it, not better than it.

To quote Luther Standing Bear, Chief of the Oglala, Lakota (1905):

From Wakan Tanka, the Great Spirit, there came a great unifying life force that flowed in and through all things — the flowers of the plains, blowing winds, rocks, trees, birds, animals — and was the same force that had been breathed into the first man. Thus all things were kindred, and were brought together by the same Great Mystery. Kinship with all creatures of the Earth, sky and water was a real and active principle. In the animal and bird world there existed a brotherly feeling that kept the Lakota safe among them. And so close did some of the Lakotas come to their feathered and furred friends that in true brotherhood they spoke a common tongue. The animals had rights — the right of man's protection, the right to live, the right to multiply, the right to freedom, and the right to man's indebtedness — and in recognition of these rights the Lakota never enslaved an animal and spared all life that was not needed for food and clothing. This concept of life and its relations was humanizing and gave to the Lakota an abiding love. It filled his being with the joy and mystery of living; it gave him reverence for all life; it made a place for all things in the scheme of existence with equal importance to all. The Lakota could despise no creature, for all were of one blood, made by the same hand, and filled with the essence of the Great Mystery. In spirit, the Lakota were humble and meek. "Blessed are the meek, for they shall inherit the Earth" — this was true for the Lakota, and from the Earth they inherited secrets long since forgotten.

Their religion was sane, natural, and human. The old Lakota was wise. He knew that a man's heart away from Nature becomes hard; he knew that lack of respect for growing, living things soon lead to a lack of respect for humans too. The old people came literally to love the soil, and they sat or reclined on the ground with a feeling of being close to a mothering power.[50]

Engagement with nature: Go outside

This module has been devoted to nature as teacher, and like every good teacher, nature creates conditions conducive to learning. As you begin to learn from nature and grapple with these new concepts, be sure to go outside now and then — go out into nature in whatever form it is locally available to you; take a walk, sit down, take a deep breath or two, and notice how your thinking changes. If you are in an urban environment, notice how nature is still there. Look at the things you do not normally pay attention to: a tree in the street, a "weed" growing through the cracks on a pavement or the pigeons (they are wild animals). Look at the sky. Feel the sun, the wind or the rain on your skin. Really notice these things, in detail.

Studies have shown that the human brain performs at a higher level after going for a short walk outside, and at an even higher level if that short walk is in a natural area. Your senses and brain have evolved to be responsive and productive outdoors, not sitting in front of a computer screen or in a windowless, air-conditioned meeting room. Try taking your next business meeting outside, or meeting a colleague and going for a walk and talk. Try taking your laptop outside. Let your human nature align with nature and notice how inspiration comes almost immediately. If you look online for definitions of the word "inspiration," you'll find:

Arousal of the mind to special unusual activity or creativity.
A sudden intuition as part of solving a problem.
Divine guidance: a special influence of a divinity on the minds of human beings; arousing to a particular emotion or action.

This is exactly what your business needs in these transformative times —
and exactly what you get when you connect with nature. Experiencing a
deep sense of connection to the natural world was our natural state for
the majority of human history; it is what shamanism is.

The characteristics of an organization that is best able to adapt, swim
with the stream of life and work with the grain of nature are the characteristics of a firm of the future — a business inspired by nature. These
are explored in detail next in Modules Three and Four. Likewise, the behaviors that best equip the individual, the leader, to be fully connected
and swim with the stream of dynamic non-equilibrium are explored in
Module Five.

Questions

1. How would you describe your personal relationship with nature?

2. How often are you able to spend time in natural environments?

3. Do you, personally, feel like you are part of nature? If so, how do you connect with nature? If not, try to explain how you are separate from nature.

4. Can you envisage having a walk through a park with a colleague or client, and the meeting–conversation being better for it?

5. Next time you get stuck on a difficult challenge, go out into a natural area for a walk and think about the challenge. Did you find it helped gain a greater sense of clarity?

6. If you were to plant seeds of inspiration for new ways of operating in your organization, how and where would you plant them?

7. Can you think of (or find) examples of other organizations similar to yours that are gaining inspiration from nature?

8. Do you feel your organization can gain inspiration from nature? How would you go about connecting people in your organization with nature's inspiration?

9. How easy is it for you to view your organization as a living being/organism? If you viewed it as a living being, how emergent would you say it is?

10. Think about which parts of your organization (and business ecosystem) are at different stages of their own ecological succession cycle (growth, conservation, release and renewal). How does your organizational culture view these different stages?

11. What are all the interactions your organization depends on with nature for its own well-being and survival (e.g., energy, food, light, water, materials, waste and emissions assimilation, customer livelihoods)? Make a list of them all. How aware do you think your organization is of this dependence?

12. How would you describe the relationship your organization has with nature? For example, does your organization have a mutually beneficial relationship with nature? Does it give something beneficial and non-toxic back to nature? How might you change this organizational relationship with nature to enhance value to your business and to nature?

13. Can you imagine your organization — or our economy as a whole — ultimately sustaining if it continues to ignore (or chooses to be ignorant of) the limits and constraints of nature?

14. Can you imagine what your business — and the economy as a whole — would look like if we all understood the materials, methods, principles and practices of nature?

Firm of the Future

> Adversity reveals genius,
> prosperity conceals it.
>
> — Horace

EXECUTIVE SUMMARY

- Businesses are recognizing the need to transform beyond the current prevailing paradigm of short-term profit maximization.
- Business is fundamentally about value creation — the how and why of value creation is itself transforming as our world and livelihoods transform.
- The increasingly volatile, dynamically transforming business environment means businesses need to behave like emergent, living organisms in order to thrive and survive.
- A firm of the future is a business inspired by nature — one that is resilient, optimizing, adaptive, systems-based, values-led and life-supporting.

One of the more devastating theories of the 1970s was that no matter what it took to achieve it, the primary purpose of business was to maximize value for its shareholders. This principle has led to a variety of social ills where businesses discard employees (at the drop of a hat), pollute our air and waters, or create short-term gains that are unsustainable. It is important for people in business to recognize that long-term shareholder value is more likely to be created by companies that value their employees, act as good environmental stewards and think long-term in general.

— RICHARD BRANSON[1]

Organizations are increasingly exposed to dynamic change: change upon change upon change — while dealing with one change, another affects us, then another, and so on. This dynamic change upsets the traditional business paradigm we have been working to over the last few decades. It is no longer appropriate to simply "manage" change through traditional change management methodologies or "manage" risk through tried and tested risk management techniques. We need to look deeper to successfully operate in these turbulent times; to transform our organizations from firms of the past to firms of the future.

First, let us share an understanding of what we mean by the terms "business model" and "business ecosystem," as they are fundamental to our exploration into the firm of the future.

Business model

The business model of the organization is its approach to providing value for its stakeholders. Thus, the organization's understanding of what it means by "value" and what it means by "stakeholder" is fundamental. Value tends to be defined in terms of monetary profit (as money has become the currency for expressing exchange of value, hence gaining more money for something can mean more value has been gained). If we step back from money as a value exchange mechanism and look deeper into what constitutes value, we see that organizations rely on resources and relationships to generate and sustain value. The availability of such resources and relationships affects the viability of the organization to generate value in the short, medium and long term. The relationships the organization has with its stakeholder community are connected across its business ecosystem (see page 76). A stakeholder is any person or group of people who interrelate with the organization. For example, a stakeholder could be a supplier, an employee, a customer, a partner, a distributor, a regulator, a trade union, a pressure group, a trustee, an investor, and so on.

Value, relationships and resources have both quantity and quality aspects, and we can seek to quantify them by using "capital." Capital here, in relation to our prevailing economic paradigm, refers to stock from

Extract from interview with Paul Polman, CEO of Unilever[2]

When Polman announced his intention to abandon earnings forecasts, Unilever's shares dropped 10 percent at a stroke. "I do not wish to be political, but my decisions are made in the long-term interests of the company. It would be easy for me to jack the share price up, collect a bonus and go sailing in the Bahamas, but in five or ten years Unilever would not be in good shape... It is clear to me we are coming out of the financial crisis and into a "new normal," created by tremendous pressure on the resources of the Earth. There are two billion more people coming in the emerging markets and standards of living there will rise," adds Polman. Polman believes the "new normal" requires a different approach to doing business, codified in his strategic brainchild, the "sustainable living plan" with three key objectives, to be achieved by 2020: to cut the environmental impact of Unilever's products in half by slashing water use and carbon emissions; to source sustainably all its agricultural supplies; and to improve the health and well-being of a billion people worldwide. Oh, and to do all this while doubling sales revenues.

"Too many people think in terms of trade-offs," Polman says, "that if you do something which is good for you, then it must be bad for someone else. That's not right and it comes from old thinking about the way the world works and what business is for: Milton Friedman's optimization of short-term profits. We have to snap out of that old thinking and move to a new model.

"Our new business model will decouple growth from environmental impact. We will double in size, but reduce our overall effect on the environment. Consumers are asking for it, but governments are incapable of delivering it. It is needed for society and it energizes our people—it reduces costs and increases innovation."

Hence his novel campaign to "reprofile" Unilever's shareholder base, to win over the long-term investors he believes his company deserves. "We spend a lot of time disengaging from shareholders who do not benefit our strategy, and attracting those who do buy into what we are doing. There will always be people driven by short-termism, greed and self-interest, but we'd rather not have them associated with our company."

which a return can be made. The stock, or capital, can be physical or virtual. Some forms of capital are more easily quantified (and so monetized) than others. Note that the "six capitals" model below alludes to, but does not attempt to define or quantify, the more intangible qualities fundamentally important to the workings of an effective business; for example, the qualities and feelings in relationships associated with empathy, belonging, self-worth, mutual respect, trust, happiness, freedom and love. Such intangible qualities are important aspects of business life (especially these days with the blurring of boundaries in business, social and personal life).

The six "capitals" are: financial capital, manufactured capital, human capital, intellectual capital, natural capital and social capital.[3]

Financial capital: Funds obtained through generated operations, investments or financing, and used in the production and provision of products and services.

The organization positively impacts financial capital by earning more money than it spends, invests or owes. Vice versa, it negatively impacts financial capital by owing or spending more money than it earns. In our debt-based economy, the prevailing business ethos is to borrow financial capital against future earnings, and so the amount owed accrues based on predicted future financial earnings and predicted future growth in those financial earnings. Investors (shareholders) often desire returns on their investment in the short term, encouraging the organization to meet short-term financial returns through higher earnings and/or lower investment. The need to meet shareholder returns and finance accruing debt propagates the need for increased financial returns beyond just investing in the other forms of capital. In this regard, financial capital, as well as acting as a medium for investment of value accrued from one form of capital to another, also services external debts and shareholder commitments. In this case, financial capital can be extracted from the organization (due to an agreed repayment debt/investment provision), rather than being invested in other forms of capital for the organization to increase its value-creation potential.

Manufactured capital: Manufactured physical objects used in the production and provision of products and services (e.g., buildings, equipment, infrastructure).

The organization positively impacts manufactured capital by investing other forms of capital into the manufacturing of such buildings, equipment and infrastructure, which in turn are aimed at helping generate higher returns for the other forms of capital. Vice versa, it negatively impacts manufactured capital by reducing investment and maintenance of buildings, equipment and infrastructure.

Human capital: People's skills and experience, and their motivations to innovate, including the governance framework, ethics, loyalties and ability to understand and implement strategies.

The organization positively impacts human capital by investing other forms of capital into the advancement of people's skills, motivations, ethics and behaviors (e.g., financial capital toward education and training, or manufactured capital for technological improvement releasing people from laborious tasks to more creative activities). We know human skills, motivations, ethics and behaviors can be enhanced through inspirational leadership and empowerment. Hence, human capital improvement comes not just from increased investment through other forms of capital, but through inspirational and empowering human behaviors. In other words, humans can generate human capital without solely depending on other capital investments.

Vice versa, the organization negatively impacts human capital by either reducing investment in it or by reducing positive behavior that inspires and feeds more positive behavior. If a good culture is not upheld and encouraged, and self-motivating greed-fuelled forces start to undermine the organization's ethos, the collective human capital is negatively impacted. Often, the need to meet short-term shareholder returns can encourage over-exploitation of some stakeholders (increased working hours, more aggressive KPIs, for example); this is human capital viewed in terms of "sweating the assets." This has a longer-term detriment to the organization through the erosion of human capital, as sweating the human assets not only reduces the rate of return from the human capital, after a potential short-term increase, it also erodes the underlying asset base of the human capital. Put in simpler non-capital terms, getting more out of people works for a short period, but if the organization's governance seeks to over-exploit its people, then ethics, loyalties and the ability to empower, lead, collaborate and implement strategies become reduced. This is an example of short-termism undermining the organization's long-term value-creation potential.

Intellectual capital: Intangibles that enhance value through competitive advantage. For example, intellectual property (such as patents, copyrights, software and organizational systems), procedures and protocols, and intangibles associated with the organization's brand and reputation.

The organization positively impacts intellectual capital by investing in the sources of intellectual capital (e.g., human capital) and in the mechanisms to convert the sources into intellectual capital (legal agreements, standards, procedures). Vice versa, it negatively impacts intellectual capital by reducing the sources and/or rate of conversion. If human capital is being undermined, for example, through selfish behavior, to the detriment of the collective work ethic and shared intelligence, intellectual capital becomes negatively impacted. Likewise, if short-term shareholder returns and financial capital growth are prioritized to the detriment of the collective work ethic, investment in people and stakeholder relations, the organization's brand and reputation can be placed at risk of being negatively impacted if such behaviors are exposed to the wider stakeholder community.

Natural capital: The input to the production and provision of products and services (e.g., water, land, minerals, forests and wider ecosystem services).

Natural capital still remains largely unquantified; hence the work of The Economics of Ecosystems and Biodiversity (TEEB) initiative, which seeks to define and quantify the "ecosystem services" that make up natural capital.[4] The organization positively impacts natural capital by investing in activities that enrich the health of the ecosystems that support the ecosystem services from which natural capital is being derived. For example, if the organization uses a lot of water (e.g., Coca-Cola), it may invest in water ecosystems to ensure its supply of natural capital is sustainable. Vice versa, an organization negatively impacts natural capital by consuming more than the carrying capacity of that particular ecosystem. Negative impact occurs when the ability of that ecosystem to function healthily is undermined due to the organization's extraction of natural capital from the ecosystem.

Here lies a conundrum. First and foremost, the organization often does not own the natural capital. It may or may not have obtained legal rights to access the natural capital and the ecosystem services that flow from that, yet often these legal rights do not take into account the ecosystem health and livelihood. Just as human resource policies and rights fall sometimes short in taking into account the overall (holistic) wellbeing of the person contributing to the human capital, rarely do the rights to extract natural capital from nature take into account the overall well-being of the ecosystem. This incompleteness is to the detriment of the long-term health of this capital-based approach to business. In the short term, the organization may benefit from exploiting natural capital and so driving input for other aspects of the capital-based business model, but in the longer term it is negatively impacting the source of that natural capital. While the work related to quantifying ecosystem services makes ground in the quantification of natural capital, incompleteness still abounds.

> Intangible values, which may be reflected in society's willingness to pay to conserve particular species or landscapes, or to protect common resources, must be considered alongside more tangible values like food or timber to provide a complete economic picture. Valuation is seen not as a panacea, but rather as a tool to help recalibrate the faulty economic compass that has led us to decisions that are prejudicial to both current well-being and that of future generations. The invisibility of biodiversity values has often encouraged inefficient use or even destruction of the natural capital that is the foundation of our economies.
>
> — THE ECONOMICS OF ECOSYSTEMS AND BIODIVERSITY (TEEB)[5]

Social capital: The relationships and networks between stakeholders, including common values and behaviors, the trust and loyalty the organization has built up across its stakeholder community, and the organization's social license to operate.

The organization positively impacts social capital by investing in stakeholder relations and building a social environment of trust and loyalty, which fosters openness, trust, sharing and mutualism within and beyond organizational boundaries. This in turn positively impacts the people (human capital) and the organization's brand and reputation (intellectual capital). Vice versa, it negatively impacts social capital by allowing (or even encouraging) behaviors that weaken social bonds and relationships. For example, over-competitive, parasitic and exploitative behaviors that seek to maximize the short-term return of one party at the expense of another will lead, in the long term, to a degradation of social capital and, in turn, human capital and intellectual capital.

Hence, competition can (if unchecked) undermine social and human capital (and so, in turn, intellectual, manufactured and financial capital). Collaboration, rather than rampant competition, is more constructive a force for generating social and human capital (and so, in turn, intellectual, manufactured and financial capital). However, it is also worth noting that competition (if checked and balanced) can help stimulate motivation and innovation, and hence, in turn, contribute constructively to social and human capital. It is a balance of collaboration and competition that needs to be found, and that harmonic may alter depending on economic, social and environmental factors which may vary depending on the circumstance. Hence, being tuned in to what is fit for purpose for the situation is paramount.

While this capital-based approach to understanding the business model does not fully represent the holistic, emergent and interrelated nature of business, we can see from this approach that there are interconnections between the capitals. For example, manufactured capital may need human capital, natural capital, financial capital, intellectual capital and social capital to grow. Also, for example, financial capital can be eroded if human capital, natural capital, social capital, manufactured capital and intellectual capital are neglected. While a capital-based approach may seek to reduce the whole into parts in order to help categorization and understanding, we can see how the parts interrelate to each other, and that those interrelationships can be mutually beneficial (one capital improvement leading to an improvement in another capital) or parasitic (one capital improvement leading to a decline in another capital).

This capital-based modelling approach has been well explored in relation to challenging the prevailing business paradigm. I make particular reference here to two areas of work worth closer examination by the reader:

+ Jonathon Porritt and Forum for the Future's work, as referred to in his book *Capitalism as if the World Matters*, a book I strongly recommend reading (of particular relevance here is part 2, pp.135–210).[6]
+ HRH The Prince of Wales's Accounting for Sustainability Project, the International Integrated Reporting Committee and the *Accounting for Sustainability* book by Hopwood et al., which all explore how economic, social and environmental aspects of business can be integrated through reporting.[7]

As said, business is first and foremost about value creation and providing value to the customer, and as such it does not have to be defined in terms of capital and profit. Here are some of the important aspects that ought to form part of a successful business model (a non-exclusive list):

+ Organizational goal/mission, and the values and strategy to achieve that goal or mission — the why, how and to whom it is adding value.
+ Organizational culture — an understanding of how the values drive behaviors.
+ Stakeholder community map — an understanding of the key stakeholders associated with the organization, their own objectives, values and relationship potential with the organization.
+ Target customer base — an understanding of the customer groups, types and relationship potential with the organization.
+ Partner ecosystem — other organizations and stakeholders who help deliver the organization's mission and generate value potential.

- ◆ Core competency — the essential capabilities and tools to deliver the mission.
- ◆ Value proposition — the market offer to the customer and/or partner. This consists of the way in which the product or service is marketed, bundled and delivered to the customer, the pricing strategy, the delivery channel strategy and the customer value. The organization can have multiple value propositions, especially if it has a portfolio of diverse products and services and/or diverse market activity.

There is an interesting relationship here between values (inherent in the mission and culture of the organization and its respective stakeholders) and value (inherent in the mission and value proposition). There is no such thing as a person devoid of values; we all have a value set, which drives our behaviors in business and beyond. Some values and behaviors encourage good business; others encourage bad business. Likewise, organizations exhibit values and behaviors through their prevalent culture. We shall revisit this relationship between values and value shortly, as it is fundamental to the health and viability of the firm of the future.

Business ecosystem

All organizations operate within a community — an environment of interconnections. The age-old adage "no man is an island" is the same for an organization. In fact, just like an ecosystem in nature, the more diverse the relationships and resources an organization makes use of, the more resilient it becomes. The organization is, in effect, surrounded by a semi-permeable membrane that provides a porous boundary between the internal organization (where the internal stakeholders and resources reside, those directly employed or "owned" by the organization's legal entity) and the outside organization's business environment of external stakeholders and resources that interrelate with the organization as separate entities.

In these days of globalization and digitization, this semi-permeable organizational boundary is not limited by geography. While the organization has physical sites and discrete markets it may operate in, its internal stakeholders can work for the organization (within its organizational boundary) while located anywhere around the globe. In fact, it is normal these days for an employee, while on holiday or over a weekend, to dip into the organizational boundary to check emails, dial in to a conference call, take part in a WebEx meeting or meet someone (prearranged or by accident) where the conversation relates to the goals and purpose of the organization that person works for. In fact, these days, it is less about working for an organization and more about working with an organization — contributing to the success of its value-creation potential and, in so doing, also contributing to the success of the individual's value-creation potential.

More and more, organizations attract and retain employees that fit their culture and objectives. The more organizations transform to firms of the future, the more the internal stakeholder's value-creation potential (however diverse) aligns with the organization's value-creation potential — this is good business sense.

As this transformation of the organization occurs, the more this sharing of core values and behaviors spreads to external stakeholders. The more open and responsive the organization, the more boundaries between internal stakeholders and external stakeholders blur. This blurring of boundaries is encouraged and facilitated through trust, which comes from a mutual understanding of each other's values and objectives. It is this interconnection of relationships across the organization's semi-permeable membrane that provides resilience, adaptation and responsiveness. The "business ecosystem" consists of all the resources and relationships interconnected with the organization's mission and value-creation potential. In turn, the organization's business model must also accommodate and recognize the interconnectedness of relationships and resources throughout this business ecosystem.

As with keystone species and niche species in nature, business ecosystems can comprise keystone organizations and niche organizations. Keystone organizations may control assets — distribution, technology or brand — that are vital to their ecosystems. However, as in nature, the ecosystem gains greater resilience through greater diversity of asset distribution (web connections) and organization type (species diversity). So organizations that are keystone within their ecosystem instead of seeking greater control should seek greater distribution and shared contribution (co-creation) with partners, improving the resilience of the overall ecosystem, and hence their own resilience.[8] This "letting go" of control to benefit the whole (and so in turn the organization) is a great challenge for many on the transformative journey toward the firm of the future.

> Apple and Tandy were competitors in the IT industry. Tandy was vertically integrated, controlled the whole value chain and discouraged any independent initiative outside of its control. It ultimately stifled its own ecosystem, whereas Apple encouraged independent players to join its ecosystem and leveraged their innovations.[9]

In their book *What We Learned in the Rainforest*, Tachi Kiuchi and Bill Shireman explore organizations in terms of developmental succession stages of innovation, growth, improvement and release.[10] These stages align with nature's ecosystem succession stages, covered in Module Two. Kiuchi and Shireman insightfully point out the organization is constantly evolving through these stages at different rates and different ways within its business (and, of course, so too its wider business ecosystem). Learning to become aware of the stage that part of the organization (and business environment) is in will help ensure that leadership, management and investment approaches can be tailored accordingly. As explained in Module Two, the more capable the organization is at encouraging multiple ecological succession flows in its organization and wider ecosystem, the more resilient the business is.

Business and nature

As we have gathered by now, inspiration for the current pressing challenges is all around us in nature. Nature has been dealing with dynamic change for over 3.8 billion years, and the more we explore and connect with nature's ways, the more we find inspiration for operating in a dynamically changing business environment.

Our understanding of nature has evolved over the last few decades, from viewing nature as a battleground of competition to one of dynamic non-equilibrium, where an order within chaos prevails due to unwritten natural patterns, feedback loops, behavioral qualities, interdependencies and collaboration within and throughout ecosystems. Nature adapts within limits and creates conditions conducive to life. Recent discoveries in microbiology and quantum mechanics uncover the importance of cellular membranes in the adaptation and evolution of organisms. Likewise, the perceptions and beliefs of the individual, organization and ecosystem can affect their ability to sense, respond, adapt and evolve to volatility in their environment.

The more we grapple with the challenges our businesses now face in these volatile times, the more we realize that nature's patterns and behaviors can inspire approaches for our own evolutionary success in business and beyond. The more we build a bridge between business and nature, the more we realize what good business sense really is.

Nature's business principles

Biomimicry for Creative Innovation (BCI), a collaborative of specialists applying ecological thinking for business transformation, has developed a set of business principles for the firm of the future, developed from the "life principles" created by the Biomimicry Institute.

These business principles build on a wide set of existing business theories[11] and are not aimed at providing perfection in organizational design (if such would ever exist). They provide a framework to guide successful transformation toward a firm of the future — a business inspired by nature.

Such business principles are aimed at creating business conditions conducive to collaboration, adaptability, creativity, local attunement, multifunctionality and responsiveness; hence, enhancing the evolution of organizations from rigid, tightly managed hierarchies to dynamic living organizations that thrive and flourish within ever-changing business, socioeconomic and environmental conditions. Organizations that understand how to embed these principles from nature into their products, processes, policies and practices create greater abundance

Business principles for the firm of the future

Build resilience: It's more effective to build resilience than to correct poor risk-based decisions that were made with partial information. A business inspired by nature builds resilience by:
- Using change and disturbance as opportunities rather than fearing them as threats.
- Decentralizing, distributing and diversifying knowledge, resources, decision-making and actions.
- Fostering diversity in people, relationships, ideas and approaches.

Optimize: Optimizing delivers better results than maximizing or minimizing. A business inspired by nature does this by:
- Creating forms that fit functions, not the other way around.
- Embedding multiplicity into both functions and responses.
- Creating complexity and diversity using simple components and patterns.

Adapt: Being adaptive pays back better than "staying a fixed course." A business inspired by nature adapts by:
- Creating feedback loops to sense and respond at all levels of the system.
- Anticipating and integrating cyclic processes.
- Being resourceful and opportunistic when resource availability changes.

Integrate systems: With limited resources and a changing environment, it's better to be systems-based rather than independent. A business inspired by nature works with whole systems by:
- Fostering synergies within communities.
- Fostering synergies within energy, information and communication networks.
- Creating extended systems to continuously recycle wastes into resources.

Navigate by values: In uncertain times, it's better to be based on a compass of values than a fixed destination point or set of predefined metrics. A business inspired by nature reflects values by:
- Knowing what's really important to the communities in which it operates, interacts and impacts.

- Using values as the core driver toward positive outcomes.
- Measuring what is valued rather than valuing what is measured.

Support life: In the long run, it takes less effort and less resources to support life-building activities than to be damaging or toxic and pick up the cost later. A business inspired by nature supports life-building activity by:
- Leveraging information and innovation rather than energy and materials.
- Creating support for individual components that can support the whole ecosystem; supporting the ecosystem so that it can support the individual.
- Making products water-based, renewable, bio-based and biodegradable.

for themselves and their business ecosystems in times of rapid change, flourishing rather than perishing in volatile business conditions. Organizations inspired by nature are resilient, optimizing, adaptive, systems-based, values-led and life-supporting.

Let's explore each of these business principles.

Resilient

Resilience is the ability to withstand unpredictable shocks. The more resilient an organization is, the more able it is to successfully deal with disturbances and volatility. Hence, resilience is fast becoming the Holy Grail for businesses in these increasingly volatile times.

Decentralization, distribution and diversity within the people, process, product and places aspects of a business help develop resilience. The more diverse, decentralized and distributed the business and its business ecosystem, the more able it is to seek out opportunities and capitalize upon a changing business landscape.

In nature, we find inspiration for resilience within flourishing ecosystems. Take a forest, which maintains different development stages within its ecosystem. Some parts of the forest are in a state of rapid growth or regrowth, while other parts are maturing, and yet others are

Adnams (a UK Brewery) recently shifted their focus from a few product lines and customers to increasing the diversity of products and their customer base. The shift toward a greater variety of products and customers led to investment in adjacent markets. During this business transformation, Adnams also invested in its employees, ensuring they became more empowered to make decisions locally, hence reducing the need for overly burdensome centralized management. These changes have significantly increased Adnams' resilience, leaving them far better equipped to deal with market volatility and seek out new opportunities.

fully mature and aging. There is continual cycling through these stages, with disturbances (such as fire, flood or storm damage) driving release of resources, which in turn leads to reorganization and regrowth (akin to new products being launched and new ways of working being introduced). By maintaining constant cycling at different scales of time and space, the forest is able to flourish during short-term disturbances as well as long-term change. Diversity is key to nature's success.

Optimizing

While maximization brings benefit of economies of scale through lower unit cost of production, in nature we find optimization through economies of scope brings different benefits through improved cross-fertilization and species interaction (akin to improved interactivity across traditional department and organizational boundaries). Maximization is driven through homogenizing, scaling up, atomizing, industrializing and reducing complexities within a specific business function, system or process; optimization is driven through enhanced connections, interactivity and interdependencies across different business functions, systems or processes.

Economies of scale rely on mass production, which can reduce the potential for synergies in an organization; reducing the variety of products curtails creativity and innovation, can lower staff engagement levels, ultimately weakening the company's overall resilience. Economies of scope realize benefits by unlocking synergistic win–win relationships and positive virtuous cycles, increasing co-creation through increased interconnections across the wider business ecosystem. This increases the system's overall resilience and improves the ability to optimize. It is not that maximizing or economies of scale are not good; it is more that the right balance between maximization and optimization needs to be found, where the benefit from scale is balanced by the benefit of scope, thus ensuring the best delivery of services or products in any given market at any given time.

> Just prior to the economic crisis, Adnams reorganized into more separate, siloed business units. At a time when rapid change and collaboration were needed, to deal with the external threat of the global crisis, it quickly sensed the reduction in synergies brought about through the separation of business functions and the reduced collaboration between parts of the business. Responding to this quickly, it returned to a more integrated functional approach, where economies of scope were realized more readily through interconnections between stakeholders and the fostering of local empowerment.

In nature, we see that the ability for organisms to cooperate, optimize and synergize within their environment is fundamental to their successful evolution. As discussed in Module Two, life is not simply a competitive struggle; rather, it's an interwoven interplay of cooperative partnerships. In nature, economies of scope are fundamental for adaptation and survival. It is species that have multiple synergistic interconnections within their ecosystem that co-create resilient ecosystems more able to thrive in dynamic change.

> Unilever is undertaking significant adaptation across its business, not just in the way it sources, produces and distributes products but also in the way it engages stakeholders across its entire business ecosystem. It is adapting its business approach to become fit for purpose within the business environment in which it now operates.

Adaptive

According to Charles Darwin's theory, it is not the strongest species that survive, nor the most intelligent, but the ones most able to adapt to change.

The ability to leverage stakeholder feedback is an important factor that enhances organizational adaptiveness. Hand in hand with sensitivity to stakeholder feedback is attunement to social, economic and environmental trends (macro and micro). Sensing and responding to market signals is a hallmark of innovative, adaptive organizations. Adaptive organizations seek sources of innovation from customers, suppliers and the public, in addition to internal employees and traditional R&D sources (exemplified by Proctor and Gamble shifting from "research and development" to "connect and develop," to encourage innovative ideas from external sources). More recently this external stakeholder connection is being facilitated through "open-source innovation platforms" (explored in Module Six).

General Electric (GE) is adapting and transforming its business strategy and operations toward products and services that enhance the sustainability and long-term value of its customers and wider stakeholder community, sensing this is where the future lies. "Ecomagination" puts into practice GE's belief that financial and environmental performance can work together to drive company growth, while taking on some of the world's biggest challenges.[12]

Adaptation is enhanced when the organization (individuals and communities of stakeholders) finds it easier to let go of the old and embrace the new. For example, geese flying in a V formation rotate leadership to ensure that at any given point in the journey, leadership is always fit for purpose. As we explore in Module Five, leadership that encourages adaptation helps ensure success in firms of the future.

Systems-based

While reducing complex problems, projects or production lines into small, manageable chunks has the advantage of simplifying management and control, and enabling economies of scale to be gained through industrialization, it can reduce the interconnections and interdependencies between activities that give rise to synergistic value enhancement.

Business, like nature, is lit up by interconnections and relationships that find success by being both system-focused and self-focused. Whatever the organization (or organism) does to benefit itself should also benefit the system; in benefiting the system, it also benefits itself. In business, organizations enhance a "systems approach" by developing and maintaining networks of relationships among diverse partners.

In nature, fungi provide an interconnected web of life in the soil beneath our feet, breaking down plant waste and stones into food for plants, and feeding the plants while also gaining food from them (completing the circle of life). Scientists have often been baffled by how certain species grow in certain conditions within their natural habitat, but when put in the same conditions within a laboratory fail to survive. Recently, through radioactive tracing of nutrient flows, scientists found that through fungi (mycelium networks) in the soil, nutrients from one part of the forest (where perhaps there is more sunlight, for example) are fed to plants in another part of the forest. The fungi distribute and share nutrients between different parts of the ecosystem as the health of the overall ecosystem benefits the whole, the parts and, in turn, the fungi. It is in the fungi's interest to be part of a healthy, resilient ecosystem, just as it is in the organization's interest to be in a healthy, vibrant business ecosystem and social community.

Novo Nordisk, a Danish healthcare and pharmaceuticals company, uses a multistakeholder approach to help develop collaboration and participation among a wide range of stakeholders. The approach is based on a reflective understanding of others' positions and motives, realizing that relationships are not static but ever-changing. Stakeholder engagement with a diverse set of stakeholder groups not only helps solve business issues effectively for Novo Nordisk but also provides a great source of innovation for them and their partners.[13]

The concept of partner and stakeholder ecosystems in business has been around for some years, with organizations like Cisco successfully building partner ecosystems to aid their performance. Successful partner relations can help build vital trust among stakeholders farther afield, too. As customers' and consumers' requirement for authenticity and transparency increases, so too does the corporations' need to connect and engage authentically with social and environmental stakeholder groups. Partnerships with local charities, community interest groups, NGOs and government institutions can help build this trust, break down historic barriers, help form working relationships and mobilize wider-ranging resources, which can enhance innovation and increase access to different skill types.[14]

> BC Hydro, a Canadian utility, developed a joint initiative between provincial governments in consultation with First Nations groups and the public. This joint initiative offered a collaboration approach which enabled traditional ecological wisdom to be integrated into business decision-making leading to enhanced cross-cultural learning and improved outcomes for the overall ecosystem of partners.[15]

Business leaders these days are well-advised to develop shared goals with a broad set of stakeholders.[16] Increasingly this involves collaboration with non-traditional partners such as NGOs, competitors and members of the community.[17] Developing strategic initiatives that serve both the stakeholders' communities and the organization's interests has been well articulated by Porter and Kramer around the concept of shared value, which we explore in more detail when looking at values and value in Module Four.[18]

Values-led

As the need increases to continuously change, let go of old ways, seek out opportunities and embrace the new, values become the core from which consistent good business behavior is rooted. Essentially, values are the organizational belief system acting as the integrating factor among diverse stakeholder groups (within and beyond the organization's boundaries). Traditional hierarchies of management and control inhibit the ability for organizations to adapt in rapidly changing environments. Rather than controlling the workforce, a firm of the future empowers the stakeholder community to take decisions locally, through common core business behaviors aligned according to values. It is values, rather than control mechanisms, that ensure consistency of behavior in realizing the organization's mission. Hence, values-based leadership becomes a differentiator for those organizations best able to transform toward becoming a firm of the future.

Panasonic's 2011 sustainability report states that their mission is "to contribute to the advance of world culture by working to improve society through the products we produce and sell." Their basic management objective: "Recognizing our responsibilities as industrialists, we will devote ourselves to the progress and development of society and the well-being of people through our business activities, thereby enhancing the quality of life throughout the world."[19]

Whole Foods Market's values-based vision: "Whole Foods Market's vision of a sustainable future means our children and grandchildren will be living in a world that values human creativity, diversity, and individual choice. Businesses will harness human and material resources without devaluing the integrity of the individual or the planet's ecosystems. Companies, governments, and institutions will be held accountable for their actions. People will better understand that all actions have repercussions and that planning and foresight coupled with hard work and flexibility can overcome almost any problem encountered. It will be a world that values education and a free exchange of ideas by an informed citizenry; where people are encouraged to discover, nurture, and share their life's passions."[20]

Values emerge from the collective behavior of individuals and relate to implicitly agreed social norms. As an organization transforms, values become increasingly important, to provide cohesion in the chaos of change. Some core values are listed here to act as a platform for debating values most appropriate for your organization:

* recognition of interdependence
* self-determination
* diversity and tolerance
* compassion for others
* upholding the principle of equity
* recognition of the rights and interests of non-humans
* respect for the integrity of natural systems
* respect for the interests of future generations.[21]

Life-supporting

Sustainability is fast becoming embedded into business best practice. It is now increasingly recognized that businesses which embrace sustainability as part of their strategy and operations are more resilient.

"Life-supporting" goes beyond traditional corporate responsibility (measuring, monitoring and reducing the negative impacts of the business). It is about creating the conditions conducive to life through all aspects of business activity; encouraging behaviors, products and services that seek to enhance the well-being of those within the business ecosystem (economic, social and environmental). A number of organizations are already transforming toward zero-emissions (Adnams, Puma, InterfaceFLOR and Panasonic, for example). This "reaching zero" goal is an important stage in the transformation, yet there is neither rhyme nor reason why business should be limited to the goal of reaching zero. Attaining positive value for all aspects of business activity is the true ambition for the firm of the future; where business relationships, products and services are mutually beneficial for the stakeholders, society and environment within which they operate.

> Consider this: all the ants on the planet, taken together, have a biomass greater than that of humans. Ants have been incredibly industrious for millions of years. Yet their productiveness nourishes plants, animals, and soil. Human industry has been in full swing for little over a century, yet it has brought about a decline

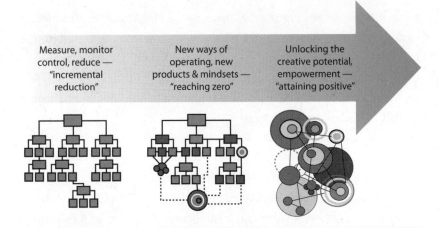

| Measure, monitor control, reduce — "incremental reduction" | New ways of operating, new products & mindsets — "reaching zero" | Unlocking the creative potential, empowerment — "attaining positive" |

Figure 6. From firm of the past to firm of the future.

in almost every ecosystem on the planet. Nature doesn't have a design problem. People do.

— MICHAEL BRAUNGART AND WILLIAM McDONOUGH[22]

Creating conditions conducive to life underpins the transformational goal of the firm of the future. It could be viewed as the most challenging of the business principles, but it is the bedrock — without it the transformational journey can lose its way in stormy seas ahead. When all aspects of the organization strive toward attaining positive value (through values), each business activity contributes toward adding value for all of life. This is the ultimate aim and the moral compass by which a firm of the future charts its transformational journey, asking itself at each step, "Does this business initiative help create conditions conducive to life?" This seems a very tall order when surrounded by the current prevailing business paradigm, yet in applying the business principles through step-by-step transformation (explored in Module Seven), the organization will find it progressively easier to challenge business activities that are not conducive to life, as virtuous cycles are formed, creating vortexes where good business sense prevails.

The transformation toward the firm of the future is a journey, not a destination. These business principles help shape the direction of the journey, yet there is no ideal business model or perfect way of operating, more it is about finding the right way at the right time for the market conditions. The future is bright for those organizations and individuals bold enough to embark on this journey of dynamic transformation — the only road to success in these volatile times.

What could a firm of the future's business vision look like? It could consist of the following aspects:

- Strategic objectives where value and values are understood as interrelated.
- Organizational culture rooted in well-being, diversity and clarity of purpose. One where individual and collective potential is encouraged through empowerment, local ownership and shared responsibility.
- A business ecosystem where there is a sense of belonging to a community of stakeholders, each having clearly understood win–win synergistic relations within the diverse ecosystem.
- Nature-inspired people, processes, products and places (infrastructure).
- Reaching to attain positive holistic value (social, environmental and economic) for all stakeholders.

From this vision and culture, a firm-of-the-future business model can evolve, where the value propositions are based on mutualism for all stakeholders (good business), rather than over-exploitation of the many for the benefit of the few (bad business).

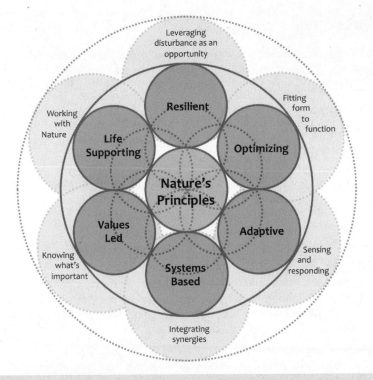

Figure 7. Nature's business principles.

Characteristics: Firm of the past ➡ Firm of the future

Find the right point along the continuum of each aspect as your organization positively adapts.

Independent	➡	Interdependent
Competitive	➡	Collaborative
Closed source	➡	Open-source
Stable	➡	Dynamic
Economies of scale	➡	Economies of scope
Resists change	➡	Leverages diversity
Linear	➡	Networked
Controlled	➡	Emergent
Self-focused	➡	System-focused
Exploitative	➡	Synergistic
Manages risks	➡	Fosters resilience
Forces	➡	Fits

Questions

1. If you were to rate your organization out of ten against each of nature's business principles, what marks would you give, and why?
   - Resilient
   - Optimizing
   - Adaptive
   - Systems-based
   - Values-led
   - Life-supporting

2. Imagine what 10/10 scoring (your ideal) for each of the principles would look like.

3. Are there organizations similar to yours that exhibit good qualities in some or all of these principles?

4. If your sole responsibility in your organization was to ensure the strategic resilience of your organization (its long-term viability), what would you do? What might be your immediate priorities as first and second steps toward this goal?

5. How would you describe the culture of your organization? What are its strengths and weaknesses? How well would it support present and future needs for transformation?

6. If you could sum up the values of your organization that characterize it for its stakeholders (customers, employees, suppliers, investors and the like), which words spring to mind? How does this compare with your competition?

7. Why would a high-performing person want to join your organization over the competition?

8. Can you start to map (or list) your organization's business ecosystem, the stakeholders and respective relations that connect them?

9. When you think of mutually beneficial relationships in your business, what springs to mind?

10. What do you see as the opportunities your organization is faced with over the next three years? What would you like your organization to be like in three years' time? Consider its structure, its culture, its value-creation potential, its market position, its values, etc.

11. Compare firm-of-the-past characteristics with those of the firm of the future in relation to your organization. Besides the obvious challenges inherent in any sort of transformation, can you think of compelling reasons why you should wish to remain with firm-of-the-past approaches?

Sustainability and the Firm of the Future

Doing business like there is a tomorrow.

— Richard Branson

EXECUTIVE SUMMARY

:» A firm of the future is one that builds a sustainable future for itself.

:» Sustainability is embedded within business transformation: strategy and operations, far beyond conventional corporate responsibility approaches.

:» In time, business ought to no longer need the term "sustainability" as it becomes ingrained into good business sense.

:» The firm of the future is not limited to just reducing its negative impact on society and the environment; it also embraces the opportunity of providing net positive value for the economy, society and environment it serves—this is real business and good business sense.

:» In looking at each aspect of the organization's business model and its business ecosystem, we see immense opportunity for positive transformation.

:» These are exciting times for good business minds.

So far sustainability has been intentionally mentioned only sparingly, as first and foremost the journey toward a firm of the future is about business survival, transformation and evolution. Organizations are in need of radical transformation due to the increasing economic, social and environmental pressures their business models are exposed to. While sustainability is part of the solution (a firm of the future), it is not the sole driving force for leaders, change agents or stakeholders embarking on radical transformation. In fact, as an organization transforms toward becoming a firm of the future, sustainability becomes a part of its DNA, its organizational makeup, just as productivity and stakeholder empowerment, for example, do.

As sustainability is a fundamentally important part of the firm of the future, let us spend some time considering what it means, how it forms part of organizational transformation, and how it is emerging and evolving as a business framework. There are lots of books, courses, conferences and research papers out there on sustainability at the moment, and the exploration here does not seek to replace the need for the reader to examine in more detail this fast-evolving, fundamentally important business topic.

> Novo Nordisk is committed to sustainable development and balanced growth. The principles of sustainable development—to preserve the planet while improving the quality of life for its current and future inhabitants—resonate well with the philosophy upon which the company was founded and how it does business today. The company "strives to conduct its activities in a financially, environmentally and socially responsible way." This implies that any decision should always seek to balance three considerations: is it economically viable? Is it socially responsible? And is it environmentally sound? This ensures that decision-making balances financial growth with corporate responsibility, short-term gains with long-term profitability, and shareholder returns with other stakeholder interests.[1]

Sustainability examines how societies and organizations can meet current human needs while not jeopardizing our future needs. Put simply, in the words of Jonathon Porritt (below), it means "living on the Earth as if we intended to stay here." Our current and future human needs are interrelated with the behavior and health of our wider ecosystem, Earth; the health of which depends upon the health of the ecosystems which make up that overriding Earth ecosystem (referred to in Gaia theory as Gaia). Gaia theory states that all life on Earth forms part of a self-regulating complex system. Earth is a system of subsystems, which all play a part in co-creating the overall health and well-being of our planet Earth. Gaia theory is now widely accepted by scientists as being an accurate representation of the way that systems on Earth, living and otherwise (e.g., weather systems), work. In an ideal world, biotic life, human society and business behavior would be mutually beneficial to each other, thriving not at the expense of the other but as a result of the other's vibrancy.

> Acting on the twin assumption that there were no limits to our natural world, and that we could lay claim to as much of its productivity and resource flow as we saw fit, the human species has opportunistically set out to colonize all but the most inhospitable habitats on Earth. In the process, we have behaved as if we were just passing through, grabbing anything we could get our hands on in the short term without any particular concern for what happens next. We have now reached the outer limits of that ecosystem, having pretty much filled up the world in the process, and are now having to think very differently given that we've got nowhere else to move on to — which means "living on the Earth as if we intend to stay here." Or, as ecologists would put it, we have to evolve out of being a pioneer species into a mature species by learning to be "self-renewing right where we are."
> — JONATHON PORRITT[2]

As said before, Earth, apart from the odd meteorite, is a closed system with respect to matter and an open energy system (solar energy from the sun continuously raining down on Earth). The Natural Step (TNS), founded by Karl-Henrik Robèrt in 1989, put forward a framework of TNS "system conditions." At the heart of these system conditions lie natural world behaviors — nature operates on continuously regenerating cyclical processes (waste of one becoming the food of another process). Here is a summary of these system conditions:

- The natural system maintains systemic equilibrium. Hence, the rate of extraction of fossil fuels, metals, minerals and such like must not exceed the rate of their safe reintegration back into the Earth's crust.

- The production and release of synthetic compounds must not exceed the rate of their safe reintegration into natural cycles.
- The basis for productivity, capacity and diversity of nature must not be diminished.
- Fair and efficient use of resources in meeting human needs.[3]

These system conditions help ensure a system balance that supports life rather than destroys life. They provide a guide as we transform toward sustainable business practices. They are not dissimilar to indigenous cultures' commandments on how to live correctly (for more information on their application to business see *The Natural Step for Business* by Brian Nattrass and Mary Altomare[4]). In the words of Mike Putman, Business Unit President at Skanska UK, "Ultimately, we want to leave the world a little better than we found it."[5]

Let us look at how our approach to sustainability in business has developed over recent years.

Stages of sustainability maturity

There are many models that explore the stages of sustainability maturity an organization goes through. In the model outlined here, compliance → cost → value → values is used to summarize the stages.

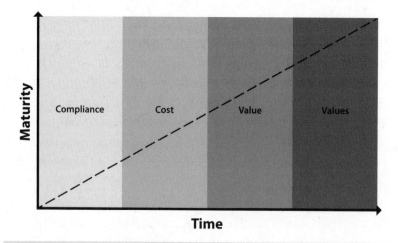

Figure 8. Stages of sustainability maturity.

Compliance

In response to legislation and tighter regulations on environmental pollution and human rights, as well as stakeholders' increased awareness about the negative effects of certain business practices, organizations embed changes aimed at measuring, monitoring, reporting and reducing negative impacts through command-and-control governance. Associated with this is the organization's need to protect its brand and reputation from prosecution and public damage. Hence, initiatives at this stage tend to be driven by fear — fear of compliance issues, health and safety issues, brand damage and so on.

Cost

As the cost of inputs (like energy) and outputs (like pollution) increase, the business case for reducing operational costs through sustainability initiatives also increases. For example, carbon reduction initiatives reduce energy and compliance costs; they also reduce the risk of bad press. While this still tends to be fear-driven at this stage, initiatives do start to generate positive effects (like cost reduction and brand enhancement) over and above risk mitigation. Such stories of cost reduction, while helping enhance the organization's brand, can also inspire stakeholders about the organization's intention to take sustainability seriously.

Value

The economic, environmental and social pressures of our perfect storm are increasing — a storm that has been brewing for some years now. As it becomes more apparent that the drivers of this storm are beyond a single economic cycle, organizations with strong leadership and conviction recognize the need to transform in the face of these challenging times. More and more business people are realizing that the changes required to survive can also bring value-creation opportunities. In fact, some would say that the perfect storm of these challenging times is exactly the right business environment in which to transform and evolve. Those stakeholders, change agents and business leaders who recognize the value-creation opportunities in embedding sustainable business into their organizations are the ones best able to evolve. According to Ray

Andersen, former Chairman and CEO of InterfaceFLOR, "My commitment to sustainability enhanced every aspect of shareholder value."[6]

This stage requires challenging the prevalent business mindset in order to explore new ways of operating, and new approaches to people, processes, products and places. Individuals, organizations and the wider stakeholder community can resist change, through fear of the unknown and blind belief in paradigms no longer fit for purpose. This stage of maturity takes courage — bold change in the face of adversity. It may be that an organization prefers a hybrid approach, where parts of the organization embed sustainability while other parts continue as before. Likewise some changes can be incremental and others transformational (challenging the status quo). This hybrid approach can help dilute the shock of more significant radical transformation, yet it can also dilute the value-creation potential realized through new ways of operating. This is a balance, with each organization needing to judge the optimal point between radical transformation and incremental change. Yet, make no mistake, the journey inevitably is toward radical transformation, as the current approach to business has expired, that much is without doubt. As is recognized by Mark Parker, CEO of Nike:

> Right now every business has a choice to make. We choose to move fast, using sustainability as a force for innovation. We choose to embrace transparency, collaboration and advocacy as tools to unlock opportunity and enable us to thrive in a clean and green economy.[7]

Elsewhere, Parker has stated Nike's intention to "prototype the future, rather than retrofit the past."[8]

At this "value" stage, the organization deeply gets that sustainability needs to be ingrained in business strategy and operations, helping drive value creation through new approaches to business as a force for innovation. Sustainability becomes part of business transformation (beyond corporate responsibility) helping enhance value and business resilience. Alignment from the board to the shop floor is required here, along with new reward systems, corporate performance reporting measures and product design and delivery approaches.

AT Kearney has noted that "companies committed to sustainability outperformed industry averages by 15 percent."[9] Similarly, according to BITC:

> Companies that consistently manage and measure their responsible business activities outperform their FTSE 350 peers on total shareholder return in seven out of the last eight years...Not only do responsible businesses fare better in strong economic times, but it seems that businesses who incorporate social and environmental factors into their core business are able to respond faster and, in this case, have bounced back from the financial crisis quicker.[10]

As new approaches to value creation emerge, so too do new ways of thinking. A new business paradigm is born; one that understands the holistic context within which the organization operates. Forward-thinking businesses are already experiencing the "breakdown" of old mindsets, giving way to a "breakthrough" of new approaches. Organizations, business schools, universities, media, institutions and pressure groups are starting to share stories of inspiration, while exposing activities still based on unsustainable old ways.

> Marks & Spencer's Plan A allocated £50 million toward implementing sustainability commitments across its business. Plan A was cost-neutral in its second year, made £50 million in 2009 and made £75 million in 2010.[11]

Values

As our understanding of our interrelated nature becomes more apparent to us, we recognize that our values as individuals, organizations, communities and even as a species are fundamentally what drive our ability to behave more sustainably, and so embrace the transformational journey. Organizations that get it are the ones that appreciate that business is less about unethical short cuts in the name of profit, and more about value creation through good business sense. Organizations and individuals (leaders and employees) that begin to walk the talk of sustainability by believing in the holistic values and mission of the organization will be those organizations that embrace this next stage of sustainability maturity.

It is a step beyond seeing sustainability as a business opportunity that can create value to realizing it is the only appropriate way to do good business, and so become intrinsic to business behavior. This is about encouraging business activity that creates conditions conducive to life and no longer tolerating activity known to be toxic to life. Unified visions, strong culture, corporate transparency and stakeholder dialogues ensure values-based sustainable business becomes everyday business. This requires a transformation in business mentality, in business models and in organizational culture.

> There are [some organizations] that are starting to radically transform themselves to be a force for good. The people in all these organizations — large and small — have the combined power of a hurricane to effect change. It should no longer be just about typical "corporate social responsibility" (or that horrible acronym CSR) where the "responsibility" bit is usually the realm of a small team buried in a basement office — now it should be about every single person in a business taking responsibility to make a difference in everything they do, at work and in their personal lives.
>
> — RICHARD BRANSON[12]

The interrelationship of values and value

Business is first and foremost about value and value creation for its respective stakeholders, in line with its mission and objectives. The primary recipient of value creation is the customer within the community of stakeholders. In this respect it is primarily the customer who benefits from the additional value the organization provides, and the value gained by the rest of the stakeholder community is derived from this. However, as explained by Vineet Nayar in his book *Employees First, Customers Second*,[13] in looking after the employees and encouraging good values and behavior, customer value naturally follows.

The John Lewis Partnership has a written constitution that sets out its principles, governance system and rules. The Constitution states that "the happiness of its members" is the Partnership's ultimate purpose, recognizing that such happiness depends on having a satisfying job in a successful business. It establishes a system of "rights and responsibilities," which places on all Partners the obligation to work for the improvement of the business in the knowledge that all share in the rewards of success.[14]

Panasonic's business philosophy is that people are the foundation of its business, so it develops people before making products.

The Virgin Group ensures quality of service by empowering employees; the Group is a commonwealth, with shared ideas, values, interests and goals. Richard Branson states clearly that "It's not about you, it's not about the business even—it's about staff and the customer."[15]

Adnams puts values first; from this flows customer value. This approach helped enable it to outperform the market with a 4 percent increase in volumes against a 4 percent market decrease. In 2011 Adnams was voted Brewery of The Year by consumers.

Organizations like Adnams, the John Lewis Partnership, Panasonic and Virgin, which promote excellence through people and values, ensure a good culture, strong brand and improved value creation. This is core to ensuring business resilience: value through values. As explored in *Built to Last: Successful Habits of Visionary Companies* by James Collins and Professor Jerry Porras, the key management principles that help leaders create significantly more shareholder return than competitors are the dedication to define core values and a sense of purpose greater than profitability alone.[16]

Peter Drucker observed that "the biggest challenge for the large company—especially for the multinational—may be its social legitimacy: its values, its missions, its vision."[17] To profit regardless of the value provided to others is to encourage business and humanity toward a downward trajectory of values and value. It ends up in what Alain De Botton refers to as "status anxiety," which is what Western (and emerging) economies are increasingly infected with today.[18] Rather than the economy generating well-being for the majority, it provides wealth for a minority and anxiety for the majority. This is not what business needs to be about. Good business is that of entrepreneurs and business people across the globe proudly and ethically applying their acumen to solving business challenges through ingenuity and dedication in order to generate value. Talented, well-rounded, values-led individuals are turned on by business and its value-creation potential, motivated to contribute their unique sparks to the economic engine for the benefit of themselves and the wider whole.

By challenging the values and value-creation potential of the organization, prevailing business mindsets and behaviors can be healthily critiqued. Only with this interrogation of values and value will business leaders understand the holistic value potential of the organization. Then, the business strategy and operations can be redesigned for resilience.

> It seems that value is created and sustainable value needs to be co-created. This brings a deeper understanding of the purpose of profit in terms of the sustainable value products, services and projects co-created. It is one thing to deliver outcomes. It is quite another to really understand and change the quality of lives... The change has been and is about creating value toward improving the quality of life.
> — TATA SERVICES[19]

Shared and holistic value

As the world becomes ever more interconnected, so too must the value-creation potential of organizations become interconnected with social, environmental and economic factors. One way to achieve more complete value is through partnerships and relationships. Blurring organizational boundaries can provide interconnecting value-creation relationships with suppliers, customers, NGOs and others. One emerging concept relating to organizational value creation is the concept of "shared value"—where economic value and social value go hand in hand.[20]

Michael Porter and Mark Kramer put forward that the purpose of organizations must be redefined with the concept of shared value — economic value and social value — which will help drive innovation and productivity. This only comes with a deeper understanding of the organization's true bases for value creation and productivity, while becoming aware of the relationships and resources that help drive value creation and productivity gain. Porter and Kramer stress that the drive for shared value does not come from philanthropy, more from self-interest, as in gaining shared value the business benefits as well as society: "The old models of corporate strategy and capitalism are dead. The new way forward is shared value. This is the new source of sustainable competitive advantage."[21]

Shared value must also include environmental value. This means the impacts and benefits the organization generates upon the environment, as well as society and the economy. Focusing on one part without the other is what leads to degradation and value destruction to the whole, hence the term "holistic value" to reflect value that incorporates social, environmental and economic value.

This holistic approach to value ensures two important aspects are dealt with correctly for the firm of the future:

1. The values of the organization are congruent with the value-creation objectives of the organization (social, environmental and economic). This means values and value reinforce each other, and so a values-led culture drives the value-creation potential of the organization. This is fundamental to enabling local attunement, agility, empowerment and creative freedom governed by values and value focus, not by bureaucracy.

2. The value-creation potential of the organization is realized for the short, medium and long term through a deep understanding of all relationships and resources within the organization and wider business ecosystem. By rooting value creation in holistic value, the organization can walk the talk; no more need for defensive protectionism or hidden exploitation, ensuring encouragement of mutually beneficial business activities for all stakeholders.

It is this awareness of the whole, the interconnected parts and the respective limits within which we operate that is at the heart of sustainable business. Creating the conditions conducive to life through values-led business is the bright future of business.

In reevaluating and transforming the organization's strategy and approach to business operations, relationships and resources, immense opportunities for innovation and new ways of working burst forth. Synergies spawn where holistic value is unlocked across stakeholder communities, seeding virtuous cycles that feed themselves through mutually beneficial value-enhancement.

There are plenty of challenges in the world today for our creative business potential to be applied to. It is a fallacy to think that if business is not driven by the desire for ever-increasing consumption of stuff

Toyota's guiding principles to business:
1. Honor the language and spirit of the law of every nation, and undertake open and fair business activities to be a good corporate citizen of the world.
2. Respect the culture and customs of every nation, and contribute to economic and social development through corporate activities in their respective communities.
3. Dedicate our business to providing clean and safe products and to enhancing the quality of life everywhere through all of our activities.
4. Create and develop advanced technologies and provide outstanding products and services that fulfill the needs of customers worldwide.
5. Foster a corporate culture that enhances both individual creativity and the value of teamwork, while honoring mutual trust and respect between labor and management.
6. Pursue growth through harmony with the global community via innovative management.
7. Work with business partners in research and manufacture to achieve stable, long-term growth and mutual benefits, while keeping ourselves open to new partnerships.[22]

it will lose its growth appetite. It ought to lose its hedonic hunger for profit for profit's sake, replacing it with value, values and good business sense.

Organizations that align their mission and objectives, and so their strategy, culture and operations toward holistic value creation, will be the ones fit for purpose for the future. Making this transformative change now is what will separate the wheat from the chaff, those that are courageous and capable from those that are fearful and false. There are some organizations, through a philosophy inherited from their visionary founders, that have for many years been cognisant of value beyond the purely economic, although recognizing and prioritizing holistic value over short-term profit-maximization is not always easy even in such companies with an enlightened philosophy. It is the effective putting into practice of this philosophy that makes business what it is: task-driven, outcome-focused, value-enhancing; not just talk but *do*.

Organizations with philosophies that recognize value beyond the purely financial are thriving in all parts of the world (as these examples show). As we now enter an age of openness, interconnectedness and responsibility, shortcuts that benefit some at the expense of others are no longer an option.

With that understanding of values and value, let us take a closer look at what makes up the organization in transformation.

The values that guide Johnson & Johnson are known as "Our Credo" and firmly put the needs and well-being of the people the organization serves first. Robert Wood Johnson, former chairman from 1932 to 1963 and a member of the company's founding family, crafted Our Credo himself in 1943, just before Johnson & Johnson became a publicly traded company. This was long before anyone ever heard the term "corporate social responsibility." Our Credo is more than just a moral compass for Johnson & Johnson—it's a recipe for business success. The fact that Johnson & Johnson is one of only a handful of companies that have flourished through more than a century of change is proof of that.[23]

People, process, product, place

There are several ways to view an organization in its completeness. Here we use the categories of people, process, product and place (infrastructure and technology), and ecosystem to help us explore components of the organization that make up a firm of the future. We have covered the business ecosystem, so now let's explore the other elements.

People

People are perhaps the most complex part of the organization. How people behave affects costs, value-creation potential and goal realization. Not only are people all different, there are different groups of stakeholders within the business ecosystem of an organization. As we saw earlier, the organization's stakeholder community can consist of a wide range of different groups of people: employees, investors, customers, suppliers, regulators, pressure groups, partners, unions, local communities and so on. Not only can people's motives and behaviors differ between stakeholder groups, but of course each individual has his or her own unique behavioral set. Hence, connecting with people, bringing them onboard and encouraging positive behavior that aligns with the organization's goals is a very important, yet complex, aspect of business transformation.

As we become more interconnected as individuals through the all-pervasive Internet (see Technology below), the working environment becomes more of an interconnected community of shared decision-making. Collective decision-making, open discussions and greater collaboration come about through this community, which in turn brings greater responsiveness to a changing environment, greater diversity in thinking and learning, and so greater resilience for the community. We discuss people (and human nature) in more detail in the next module.

Process

Processes are the series of operations through which value creation is realized. We have tried to mechanize and automate our processes where possible in order to streamline and industrialize them (for example, by allowing for economies of scale to reduce unit cost of production).

An over-emphasis on economies of scale can come at the expense of reduced benefits gained from economies of scope such as diversity, synergy and resilience. As noted earlier, the harmonic between economies of scale and economies of scope is what needs to be sought for each organization, and this will be unique to the organization, depending on its business model, ecosystem and stage of development (or ecological succession stage).

As mentioned in Module Two, industrial ecology, cradle-to-cradle and closed-looping are process approaches inspired by nature, which bring with them economies-of-scope benefits and can help the organization find its right harmonic when balanced with economies-of-scale approaches. They are the application of ecological principles to business practices and, among other things, can turn the problem of waste into an opportunity, optimizing and redesigning processes within the organization and across the value chain while creating opportunities for partnerships. Such process changes can help break down inter-organizational silos, as well as enhance external stakeholder relations. For example, a warehouse and logistics department that has numerous broken pallets and waste wood items incurs increasing waste disposal costs. Meanwhile, a supplier advises the marketing team that it is investing in biomass boilers for heat and power, and so reducing its energy costs and carbon emissions, differentiating it as a supplier. The supplier will need to purchase chipped wood to fuel the biomass boiler. Greater cross-departmental and inter-organizational collaboration, coupled with collective understanding and joint working, can help uncover such synergistic opportunities.[24]

As organizations interconnect with partners in order to provide improved "holistic value" for their customers and wider stakeholder community, so do processes need to interconnect across traditional boundaries. The need to improve holistic value means that connections with local partners become especially useful. Business processes that extend deep into local communities — where global meets local and local meets global — can help enhance local resilience and support local diversity, which in turn provides much-needed organization and business ecosystem resilience.

The redesign of sourcing, production and distribution processes is needed in the face of macro-business drivers described earlier (globalization, digitization, responsible business and pressure on finite natural resources). Business processes are undergoing fundamental change as the complete value chain of the organization is revisited through the lenses of sustainable operational excellence and sustainable innovation. Co-creation, open innovation and stakeholder-engagement approaches encourage processes to evolve from the "departmental–organizational" to the "stakeholder–ecosystem."

> Adnams invested in an anaerobic digester which turns its organic waste into energy. Adnams also has the capacity to turn waste into energy for its suppliers and local community partners too and so collects waste from them. This is a good example of industrial ecology, where Adnams' business ecosystem benefits from this cross-organization closed-looping. Such industrial ecology leads to strengthened relations across the business ecosystem where mutualism and reciprocity are encouraged.

Product

Life-cycle assessments of products have started to become the norm as manufacturers are increasingly driven by market demands to understand and manage the complete (social, environmental and economic) footprint of the products they produce.

As organizations get their heads around the complete footprint of their products, they are realizing that significant aspects of their products' embodied footprints are associated with parts of the business ecosystem (referred to as value stream when related to product life cycles) outside their organizational boundary—upstream (product suppliers, raw-material extraction and transportation to the producer) and downstream (product retailers, resellers, customer use and end-of-life disposal). Enhancing sustainable manufacturing processes within the manufacturer's organization is only part of the picture in enhancing the product's overall sustainable footprint (its overall life cycle, often referred to as "sustainable product life-cycle management").

Hence the manufacturer, in seeking to improve its products' holistic value and manage its products' complete footprints, needs to collaborate and innovate in partnership with other organizations and stakeholders in each product value stream (its life cycle). This has led to some organizations challenging whether their product is the best way to deliver holistic value to their customers and the wider stakeholder community. A number of organizations are already transforming their approach to product design, development, delivery and disposal, some organizations choosing to provide a value-based service (or solution) rather than a value-based product.

With a product approach, the customer purchases the product, uses it and often discards it when it is worn-out or obsolete. The materials and energy embedded in the product are lost to both the producer and the consumer, and there is little room for adapting the product to the customer's specific need (customization) or to the constant change in taste or technology (upgrade). The producer's business model is aimed at selling as many products as possible. Hence, having products that do wear out or become obsolete may be deemed good for the producer, as demand for new product versions is then maintained, enabling the producer to successfully continue with its business-model approach.[25] Selling a product that provides more holistic value and comes with less of a footprint may not always be good for this business model, as the customer may be asked to purchase a more expensive product that lasts longer. Providing cheaper products that do not last as long can be better for organizations with short-term profit-maximization in their sights.

With a service/solution approach, producers also become service providers seeking to enhance the longevity of their value-based relationship with customers and partners. This has been referred to as "servitization" — where the manufacturer shifts from simply producing and shipping products to producing and then providing a service to the customer. T. S. Baines and colleagues define it as follows:

> Servitization is the innovation of an organization's capabilities and processes to shift from selling products to selling integrated products and services that deliver value in use.[26]

In effect, the manufacturer sells the utilization of the product rather than the product itself. By doing this, the manufacturer retains ownership of the product (the customer just hiring it for the period agreed in the service provision agreement). Hence, the manufacturer increases the ability to manage more of the product life cycle (product maintenance, reuse, end of life, recycling, etc.) as the customer dispenses with ownership of the product, and with it the responsibility for maintaining and disposing of it. With this comes increased benefit to the manufacturer in providing a higher-quality service; hence investment up and down the product value stream is beneficial in order to improve the holistic value and reduce the complete footprint of the service provision to the customer. The sustainability credentials of the customer (the customer's footprint) improve by using the more sustainable service rather than using and disposing of the old product. Likewise, the manufacturer's suppliers can enhance their sustainability by co-innovating with the manufacturer in the provision of a more sustainable solution which benefits all parties concerned as it increases holistic value. Hence "servitization" can ensure improvements in holistic value and reductions in overall footprint, leading to better value all round for all stakeholders within the business ecosystem. Through such service innovation, industrial value chains are fundamentally reshaped, by changing the traditional roles of manufacturing and services.

The manufacturer advances its business model toward service provision, yielding more complex value relationships with customers and suppliers. This can increase resilience for the manufacturer (and customers and suppliers). For example, the manufacturer provides for the maintenance, reuse, reconditioning, recycling, waste disposal and so on. All these activities require changes to the business model, yet also provide opportunity for additional value creation (through value-adding services and longer-term service-based contracts with the customer, which can be of more value than one-off customer interactions in times of market volatility).

> In an economy of service and flow, an entire company may end up owning little or nothing but accomplishing more, while being located nowhere to sell everywhere. The more that the services

customers want can be met by efficiency, dematerialization, simplification, and lean manufacturing, the more enthusiastically those customers will be willing to pay teams of service providers. For the first time, we can plausibly and practically imagine a more rewarding and less risky economy whose health, prospects and metrics reverse age-old assumptions about growth: an economy where we grow by using less and less, and become stronger by being leaner.

— Paul Hawken, Amory Lovins and Hunter S. Lovins[27]

A simple example to illustrate the point:

Scenario 1 — product approach: The organization's goal is to provide quality carpets (product) for its customers. It designs, manufactures and delivers carpets to customers who purchase at point of delivery and then take ownership.

In seeking to enhance the holistic value of the product, the organization innovatively designs in the ability to reuse and recycle as much of the carpet as possible, while seeking to minimize transport and distribution emissions; it develops a carpet that reduces pollution and waste throughout the life cycle of the product. As the manufacturer seeks to reduce product life-cycle emissions, product life enhancement and end-of-life collection form part of the product strategy (whereas previously once the product had been sold, that may have terminated the manufacturer's associated relationship with that product). This "closing the loop" brings a lengthening of the relationship between the customer and manufacturer. This can increase complexities and costs through a longer business process and extended responsibility, and can also increase benefits gained from longer customer engagement and product differentiation. The mindset of the manufacturer shifts from focusing on producing a product that the customer wants to buy, to producing a product which is more sustainable and that the customer will be content with over its given life. Hence, there is a shift in emphasis from solely product sales and marketing to more one of customer engagement and relationship management.

InterfaceFLOR, a worldwide provider of "carpet solutions" seeks to "close the loop" with its ReEntry scheme where it reclaims as much end-of-life product as possible, thus reducing the volume that's sent to landfill. It works with local partners who can also provide other end-of-life recycling services (for example, the reuse of old office furniture).[28]

Scenario 2—service approach: The organization's goal is to provide floor covering services (solutions) to its customers.

The customer enters a service-level agreement with the manufacturer (which may also include a reseller/intermediary) where the customer is provided a certain specification and quality of service over a certain time period (with the option of value-adding extras). The service provider (manufacturer and/or intermediary) is responsible for the design, development, delivery, maintenance, customer service provision and disposal of the floor coverings associated with the service contract. Again, there is a shift in the manufacturer's mindset from producing as much quantity of product as possible to providing the best quality of service possible. The manufacturer/service provider is responsible for the holistic value of the service for the agreed time period. The customer is willing to pay more for a service contract that provides more holistic value. The manufacturer radically transforms its business model from just producer to producer and service provider.

Scenario 2 requires a shift in expectations for both the customer and manufacturer. Currently, a prevalent view among customers is that we buy and own a product, rather than hiring a service. For example, we own our own car rather than hiring a car for three years, even though hiring it with value-adding services included (such as maintenance, upgrades, etc.) and then trading it in for a more advanced model without incurring upfront capital purchase outlay may well be more sensible and profitable for customer and provider. This ownership is ingrained in the way we represent our wealth. Similarly, a prevalent view among manufacturers is that we maximize product lines rather than optimize service provision. The customer–producer relationship tends to be focused on the product quantity rather than customer retention through quality, hence the desire to invest in marketing to encourage customers to purchase more quantity.

Organizations that challenge traditional approaches through innovation and radical redesign can increase their chances of future viability.

> Xerox shifted its operation from a product-based system (selling a photocopier plus maintenance) to providing a service (selling the ability to produce copies). The service model is intended both to improve customer experience and to incentivize and enable Xerox to address the minimization of waste throughout the design, make, use and end-of-life stages.[29]

There is a challenge here, and, like anything worth attaining, it requires hard work and courage. Radical transformation of product life cycles, shifts to servitization, circular process reengineering and industrial ecology all require system change; the partners and wider business ecosystem of the organization need to be involved and cooperate in the transformation. This "system innovation dilemma" can engender resistance to systemic change as multiple stakeholders are needed to build momentum for the transformation to effectively take off. The organization needs to transform not just its operations but also its value chain and its relationships with its stakeholders (especially its customers and suppliers, but also regulators, intermediaries and so forth). The dilemma is a double-edged sword: it can encourage resistance toward transformation if the multistakeholder buy-in is weak and the conviction of the organization to transform is not resolute; yet if conviction is resolute, then the buy-in and systemic change that result drive significantly more value than incremental change on its own.

Lady luck favors the bold. It is the businesses with bold leadership, strong conviction, courage and persuasiveness that will reap the rewards. Successful systemic transformation will inspire others and fuel more systemic transformations. Incrementalism is, of course, useful to gain buy-in and prove immediate benefits through efficiency gains and "quick wins" as part of a transformational journey, but incrementalism without systemic transformation fails to change the course of the organization ("optimizing and delaying hitting the wall"), and so just delays the inevitable end game.

Place: infrastructure and technology

We have already discussed how processes are becoming more interconnected between and across organizational boundaries and how industrial ecology, servitization and cradle-to-cradle among other approaches are challenging traditional design and management approaches. Likewise, we have explored how digitization and globalization are catalyzing new ways of operating. These lead to changes in our relationship with places of work and production.

Infrastructure

The "industry of the future" is an emerging concept that is rooted in practical approaches to new ways of manufacturing, producing and operating, assisted by ecological thinking. The EPSRC Centre for Innovative Manufacturing in Industrial Sustainability, for example, is exploring with manufacturers how ecological thinking for process and plant design can help shape industries of the future.[30]

Smart grid and smart meter technologies, broadband, digital networks, communication technologies like "virtual presence," building automation systems, energy-management solutions and clean technologies are all advancing rapidly, helping catalyze changes in the places we work, be they factories, offices, retail outlets or our homes.

"Intelligent building" as a concept has been around for decades; I wrote a dissertation on it for my BSc degree in 1994, and the concept was already well established then. There is a shift afoot from viewing the place of work as a static estate to viewing it as a healthy, vibrant place that adapts and responds to the needs of the people in it (and nature around it). Truly intelligent buildings work with the grain of nature and are inspired by nature; they use the interrelationship of structure, systems, performance and design to provide an optimal working environment. Some architects, in designing and building places of work, apply a deep understanding of how the forms, colors and materials of a building affect human occupants in all their aspects (physical, emotional, mental and spiritual).[31]

Permaculture is a design system first and foremost, which is about fair share and distribution aligned with the grain of nature. While rooted in growing food, it can also be used as an ecologically sound approach to ways of living and working holistically.[32] Through intelligent design and the encouragement of connections between different parts of the interconnected system, synergies are enhanced that help drive productivity for the overall system. As a result of the intelligent design, the inputs required to drive the system reduce, with certain inputs driving parts of the system, which in turn drive other parts of the system, reducing the need for manual labor, for costly polluting mechanization or for imported goods and services.

As an intelligent nature-inspired system design, permaculture can be used not just for working with the land but also applied to ways of planning, designing and operating in communities and business. For example, the Transition Towns movement utilizes permaculture and nature-inspired design approaches for local community and business planning.[33] It seeks to encourage relationship and resource connections within and between initiatives that enhance the opportunity for synergies; intelligent design encouraging the flow of inputs from one part to another, encouraging interdependencies and greater overall value. The Transition Streets initiative, for example, seeks to encourage local business resilience while providing local vibrancy and improving community resilience. Such nature-inspired intelligent design is also very applicable for business of any size. For example, Dee Hock, founder and CEO of VISA, encouraged his business to grow the way nature does through synergies and interdependencies ensuring greater business resilience.

Technology

The role of technology in transforming new ways of operating is clearly profound. Humans, throughout evolution, have applied tools and techniques to help adapt, innovate and improve ways of living and working. We now find technology pervades almost all aspects of modern life, providing platforms for helping to transform new ways of being. The world of technology itself is going through radical transformation due to a number of emergent trends, such as social networking, smart mobility, cloud technologies, open-source technologies, co-creation and open innovation platforms. "Context-aware computing" and smart mobility technology are coming of age, where mobile devices can equip the end user in a multitude of ways, facilitating new patterns of working, while freeing workers from the burden of understanding and managing the intricacies of the technology itself—finally, then, technology is becoming properly user-oriented.

Of course, this is being aided by Generation Y (those born after 1982) being "digital natives," using social media (text, Internet, Twitter, Facebook, YouTube, Skype, etc.) as part of everyday life. The public life environment and the private working environment are also blurring as a result of this interconnectedness through digitization. A firm of the future embraces the power of social media to transform. We are witnessing an evolution from the push of traditional marketing and PR toward a dynamic dialogue of engagement between stakeholder communities, which enriches stakeholder relations in an open, collaborative and emergent way. This is more than integrating social media into the corporate website. It is about engaging dialogue in an interactive way across all channels; less about brand, more about informed, inspiring debate and engagement. This helps drive the integrity of behavior while challenging the relationships between individuals and the organization. It becomes more about emergence, expression and sharing than management and control (while recognizing that adequate system security is required within such openness). Social media are first and foremost about people and relationships. It helps drive the emergence of new ways of working, connecting and communicating in business and beyond.

Business process modelling (BPM), decision support systems (DSS), business intelligence (BI) and collaboration platforms are merging and evolving to meet the needs of organizations as they become more dynamic, open and adaptive. Stakeholders across the organization, and across the business ecosystem, need to be able to share, inform, feed back and make decisions that are interrelated with others across traditional departmental and organizational boundaries as business processes too begin to interconnect across these boundaries.

Technology has traditionally been an inhibitor of effective collective decision-making, by providing discrete data stores and business applications; now it is fast becoming an enabler for collaboration and shared decision-making through open-user interfacing and integrated platforms. Still today, due to our prevailing business management mindset of command-and-control, decision support is being talked about in terms of "horizontal" and "vertical" approaches; we are starting to recognize that it is more of a web, an ecosystem; less about dictation and more about dialogue, where the alignment to goals comes through values and mutual understanding, not from a management hierarchy. This is a big mindset change for many who have conventional ways ingrained in their approach to business; for the more forward-thinking or younger generations, this is good business sense, and the best way to flourish.

A firm of the future uses collaboration and social networking tools to drive both efficiencies in new ways of working and effectiveness through creativity and innovation. It is what Atos, a global IT service provider, refers to as "Creative: Lean" and "Collaborative: Lean," or "2C: Lean" for short.[34]

While technological advancement is an important part of our business and human evolution, we can over-rely on technology, which can obscure the interconnectedness of ourselves and nature. In the words of Jonathon Porritt:

> Our artificially constructed technosphere, however ingenious and powerful it may be, cannot operate independently of the biosphere. It is still embedded deep within that biosphere and is still subject to the laws of nature.[35]

We are living in interesting times, and businesses are transforming. It is no longer so much about the "why?" as the "how?" and even the "how radical?". Reactive "eco-efficiency" is being superseded by proactive "eco-effectiveness"; fear-based approaches are giving way to courage-led approaches, unlocking positive virtuous cycles on the road to the firm of the future, a journey that breeds abundance within limits.

> Ultimately business must restore, sustain, and expand the planet's ecosystems so that they can produce their vital services and biological resources even more abundantly.
> — AMORY LOVINS, L. HUNTER LOVINS AND PAUL HAWKEN[36]

The word "wealth" is derived from the old English word "weal," which means well-being, happiness, prosperity and welfare. It is nature's assets from which wealth creation originates; yet it is the human assets of ingenuity, resourcefulness and determination that can transform natural assets into wealth and holistic value. People are becoming more abundant, while nature's assets are under pressure, hence the need to improve our wealth creation capability in a mutually beneficial way.

These are exciting times in which to operate and innovate — business faces immense challenges and opportunities, in which we can all play an important part. The way in which individuals (as a symbiotic part of a collective organization and broader ecosystem) empower themselves and others becomes ever more important in these challenging times — and this is what the next module explores.

Questions

1   Does your organization have an emissions reduction plan in place? Is it incremental (absolute footprint reductions of up to 20 percent over the next three to five years) or transformational (40 percent or more reduction over the next three to five years)? What are the priority drivers for this reduction plan (compliance, cost, value, values)?

2. How does it feel having the knowledge that current economic activity (and probably your organization's current business activity) is having a negative impact on the world in which we live, and damaging our future livelihood?

3. How do you think it would feel to know that your work is improving society and the environment around you and the world you live in, making the future a better place not worse?

4. Do you think your organization would have a business advantage if your products, services and policies created a net positive impact on nature and society at large?

5. Can you think of any organizations similar to yours that provide products or services that could be viewed as sustainable (socially, environmentally and economically)?

6. Imagine your company becoming a firm of the future. How does it make you feel? Do you feel inspired or animated? Do you sense an entirely new world of possibilities? An unleashing of your latent creativity? Can you imagine if all the employees felt that way?

Human Nature and Nurture

Belief drives humanity.

— Bruce Lipton

EXECUTIVE SUMMARY

- Our way of working is transforming.
- Contrary to popular belief, it is not genetics but our environment that has the greatest influence on our ability to adapt and evolve.
- Encouraging and empowering people to positively adapt to a dynamic business environment is key.
- Creating a working environment that encourages learning while letting go of the fear of failure and change is also key.
- Right relations and reciprocity is wisdom handed down from ancient cultures.
- Values-based, emergent leadership is ideal for positive transformation.

Humanity is the cause of many of the pressing challenges we now face, yet humanity is also the solution. In order to explore right solutions, solutions that transform us toward a sustainable future while mitigating negative consequences, we need to take a deeper look at human nature itself.

Nature's wisdom is deep, and not fully understood by our prevailing modern culture, yet it is notable that we humans have some special attributes as a species within nature. We have self-awareness, free will and expansive intellect to innovate technological advancements and new ways of operating; we also have the potential for higher consciousness and universal understanding. We humans love to work, rest and play. We love to love, and yet burden ourselves with fear and hate. We are highly evolved, while possessing the basic instincts and urges of our primitive past.

This module seeks to cover some aspects of human nature that are fundamental for successful personal and organizational transformation. We start off by exploring the business environment with relevance to people — this fast-evolving "new world of work," as it has been referred to by some. Then we take a glimpse into the self — the human psyche and biology. Here we explore some prevailing paradigms that need examining — the role of genetics and our environment (nature and nurture) in our ability to adapt and evolve. Then we touch on organizations as groups of people, as living, learning and consciously aware organizations. We explore what leadership looks like for the firm of the future. And finally, we conclude the module with some insights into creative thinking, planning approaches and indigenous wisdom. It is hoped that in covering this vastly complex and deep area of human nature and nurture in a tractable way, one can start to examine and consider optimal human behavior for the transformation toward a firm of the future. Each of the aspects covered here in this module deserves a deeper exploration by the reader.

The new world of work

Whether we like it or not, we are becoming a global community in our ways of living and working. Young executives of today, from a variety of cultures, see themselves as belonging to a global community of humanity. The trend is increasing for globally sourced people, working flexible hours from home or remotely from site, on flexible contracts. Of course, this trend is quite understandable in the face of globalization, digitization, the opening up of labor markets and employers' need for increased flexibility. In parallel with this, surveys consistently show that Generation Y are increasingly placing social purpose, work-place culture, ethics and organizational mission as fundamentally important in their lives, as well as fair remuneration.

This "new world of work" changes the game for individuals and employers, in turn fundamentally changing the demands put on education to equip people for success. Some argue that we are on the cusp of a radical transformation in higher and further education — a paradigm shift from a siloed, hierarchical, atomized approach to education, which teaches "chunks" of subjects to its students, to a more tailored, integrated, applied, holistic approach to higher and further education, aimed at providing the adequate supply of flexible, adaptable, entrepreneurial, ethical workers and leaders that is now increasingly demanded by the global community we live in.

With community comes the recognition, awareness and valuing of diversity and local differences. Globalization without localization strips away diversity, encouraging monocultures to supersede multicultures in society and organizations. Through our desire to organize, manage, scale up, coordinate and control, we have tended toward encouraging monocultures where we seek to normalize behavior, and in turn reduce organizational (and wider socioeconomic) resilience. It is diversity that unleashes creativity; it is diversity that helps create conditions conducive for change. It is this important dynamic of "localization within globalization" that is fundamental to ensuring vital resilience for organizations able to sail these stormy seas ahead.

Within this emergent, locally attuned, diverse, interconnected community, we must find work that provides value for ourselves and others. As our global community emerges, we see the emergence of global ethics and the acceptance of (and desire for) increasing flexibility, variety and sense of purpose. The roles of human resourcing, talent management, stakeholder engagement, higher education and organizational training are evolving to meet this transformation.

In this new world of work, old mentalities and business paradigms are being challenged, not least that of business leadership. Traditionally, we have been taught that leaders are either born leaders or trained through leadership courses to become leaders. Yet as the characteristics of the individual, organization and wider working community continue to evolve, so too emerges a "third way" to leadership.

This third way does not dispute that some people may be naturally more charismatic and inspiring than others, nor that learning approaches to inspire, influence and lead people is not useful. This third way is rooted in individuals and their interconnectedness with their environment (social, economic and environmental). It starts with the self, the understanding of the self, the self-belief, the values, purpose and path of the self, and its relationship with life. From the foundation of the inner self, one then explores how best to interconnect with the wider community, and so how best to behave, inspire and lead in business and beyond. From clarity of core values comes clarity of real value — real holistic value that improves all aspects of economic, social and environmental value.

While, on the surface, diverse, interconnected, open, emergent organizations may appear more chaotic and difficult to manage, they are vibrant places for people to become self-empowered and to inspire others — self-managing through mutual understanding of correct behaviors rooted in core values and clarity of purpose. It is this shared value set of core ethics that ensures the chaotic nature of self-empowered diversity naturally emerges toward delivering the value-creation goals of the organization, while maintaining flexibility, adaptability and sense of purpose.

Due to the emergence of the new world of work, the firm of the future has no choice but to be an organization that embraces this global community, global in outlook while local in behavior — multicultural with share values. Firms of the future are organizations that are able to recognize and embrace their role within a globalized yet localized business environment; viewing their ecosystem of stakeholders as a community within which they thrive and prosper for the benefit of all.

It is worth mentioning here the immense opportunity non-profit organizations have amid this perfect storm, in partnering with for-profit organizations to help deliver their mission while helping the for-profit organization transform to a more resilient and sustainable organization. These synergistic partnerships between charities and business are on the rise and bring with them great mutual benefits for both partners, yet each partner needs to be ever-conscious of ensuring the synergistic nature of the relationship does not turn parasitic or merely philanthropic (and so miss the richness of co-creating value with a shared delivery mission). The for-profit organizations can bring first-rate project management, delivery excellence, economic acumen and much-needed targeted investment, which the non-profit can utilize for implementing its mission locally. The non-profit can bring first-rate local knowledge, hands-on deployment and engagement skills with social and environmental acumen.

No doubt the next few years will yield a bountiful supply of examples of synergistic partnerships inspiring others about the importance of non-profit organizations in improving business resilience.

Now that we have explored the emergence of the new world of work in relation to organizations and employees, let us take a look at the individual.

The self

In understanding human nature, let's take a step back and first look at the nature that makes us who we are — our biology. Let's explore some of the paradigms by which we understand human nature today, challenge them in the light of recent discoveries and see how this can help us deal successfully with dynamic changes in our environment, and so help us on our journey of transformation.

As the world-renowned cell biologist Bruce Lipton explores in his fascinating books,[1] four "myth perceptions" prevail in our view of human life:

1. Biological processes employ Newtonian physics.
2. Genes control biology.
3. Survival of the fittest.
4. Evolution is a random process.

Genes are a very important part of human behavior; they are the "blueprints" from which the proteins read. However, through more recent discoveries in the fields of microbiology and stem-cell research, we learn that it is our environment that drives the cell sensors and receptors that, in turn, provide signals that drive protein behavior, which in turn drives which DNA gene codes are copied to RNA, to create new cells and proteins to drive human behaviors. The master control for human behavior is not DNA; it is the environment within which the human operates.

The Marks & Spencer and Oxfam clothes exchange partnership has been running since January 2008, raising £3 million for Oxfam's charity work, while helping M&S realize its Plan A goals. Anyone donating an item of M&S clothing to Oxfam receives a £5 M&S voucher providing value for the customer, the partner charity and the partner business.

Unilever's three-year partnership with the National Childbirth Trust (NCT) in the latter's "nearly new sales" involves in the region of 500,000 customers and the distribution of 750,000 branded materials, while providing NCT with its largest fundraising program. NCT gains the benefit of Unilever's brand and procurement expertise, while Unilever connects with potential customers through NCT's voluntary-run events.

The Kenco Coffee Company has recently expanded its partnership with the Rainforest Alliance. The Rainforest Alliance provides expertise on sustainable farming and sourcing at a local level, helping Kenco achieve its goal to source its entire coffee range from Rainforest Alliance-certified farms, in turn aiding the charity's mission, while improving resilience of supply for Kenco.

Starbucks and the Rainforest Alliance have a symbiotic partnership. Certified coffee is grown on farms where forests are protected, and rivers, soils and wildlife conserved. Workers are treated with respect, paid decent wages, properly equipped and given access to education and medical care. Starbucks differentiate their coffee with the Rainforest Alliance seal, and improve resilience of supply through enhancing sustainability of their farmers and coffee crops. The Rainforest Alliance deliver on their mission of ensuring the farms meet demanding social and environmental standards.

Coca-Cola partners with the World Wide Fund for Nature (WWF) to help water conservation. Water is a main ingredient for Coca-Cola and is an important part of WWF's wildlife conservation mission. WWF helps Coca-Cola with watershed conservation and water-efficiency projects within its supply chain. Coca-Cola, along with WWF, promotes awareness and education on water-scarcity issues worldwide.

At the forefront of cell biology is epigenetics—the study of what is controlling gene behavior—which explores how our cells sense and respond to environmental signals and how these signals are converted ("signal transduction") from one form of environmental information into another form of biological information within cell behavior. Exciting discoveries have revealed that our genes can actually adapt during our lifetime to environmental influences and that mutations do not only occur by chance. In times of stress or challenge, when growth is inhibited, proteins focus in on the gene that is most agitated as a result of the stress, and then the genetic copying of that gene is done in a way that purposefully mutates, creating different copies of the RNA from the DNA, giving rise to mutations. This is referred to as "gene amplification," where it is the gene under stress that is amplified through mutation; in turn, new variations of the gene propagate, with the most suitable one being the one that best survives under the environmental conditions it is exposed to. Hence, stress from the environment brings innovation through purposeful mutation, causing an evolution in response to the environmental condition.

While Darwin's *The Origin of Species* remains key to our understanding of nature, more recent discoveries have added new dimensions to our understanding of evolution through random mutation. The more we understand cellular biology in parallel with quantum mechanics, the more we realize that it is not just random mutation but also adaptive mutation that drives evolution. Adaptive mutation occurs when an organism is stressed by environmental conditions, causing mutations that lead to adaptations to its environmental pressure. Far from life being a history of randomness, we see life as purposefully evolving to continual environmental changes.

The French biologist Jean-Baptiste Lamarck (1744–1829), in his theory of inheritance of acquired characteristics (first presented in 1801), noted that organisms and their environment change through their interaction with each other. Lamarck also put forward that life was a cooperative interaction with its environment—that cooperation was the primary driver for evolution rather than competition. Again, the more we understand about biology and quantum mechanics, the more we realize that Lamarck's perceptions bring important insight to the understanding of evolution. No longer can we view evolution as a random process, and no longer can we ignore the collaborative interplay of life with its environment.

Quantum mechanics is showing us how the universe and life as we know it are made up of energy fields and energy interactions between energy vibrations. Energy signals are 100 times more efficient in propagating information than physical (biochemical) signals. All life communicates through energy fields (just as shamans and indigenous elders seek to do when communicating with nature's wisdom through energy vibrations from animals and plants). We each have our own energy profiles, and we continuously emit and receive energy vibrations as we interact with our environment. Often we sense bad vibes or good vibes with places or people; this is our subconscious picking up on subtle energy changes. As we have separated ourselves from nature over the years since our animist past, we have become less able to tune into our environment, less able to perceive our surroundings and changes in our environment.

Some argue that "conscious awareness" is always available to us — ever present — and that it is only our fears, thoughts, likes and dislikes that keep us from it. If this is indeed the truth, then our perception can be our greatest challenge or greatest gift, depending on how we choose to perceive.

In human nature, it is our perception that influences our sensing and responding to our environment, and it is our perception that can influence our evolution. Our emotions, intentions, state of mind and belief system affect our perceptions, and our subconscious mind affects our conscious mind. Stress, anger and fear are like gauges on a dashboard through which we control our pathway through life, with our emotions being our feedback mechanism for understanding how these gauges are doing. By effectively dealing with stress, anger and fear, we can help deal with the deep problems of disease, depression and disorder.

There has been a lot written recently on the causes of mental health and well-being. In the words of Peter Owen Jones, "the quest for well-being plots the course humanity has taken since the beginning of time."[2] Far from it being material wealth that brings mental health and general well-being, of greater importance are: social connections; curiosity and learning; making positive impacts on others; being active; and appreciating the things around us. The Centre for Well-being at the new economics foundation, founded by Nic Marks, puts forward five ways to well-being:

1. connect
2. be active
3. take notice
4. keep learning
5. give.[3]

Nic Marks suggests that well-being is broader than just happiness; it also encompasses individual resilience. The more we have clear intention, self-understanding, self-belief and self-discipline, the more we can empower ourselves and others to adapt successfully in times of turbulence.

Cancer is becoming more prevalent in Western society. Cancer is an effect (symptom) of a deeper cause (often linked to our unbalanced, disconnected way of life). Many diseases we experience are symptoms of a disharmony within ourselves and our environment. As a human species, we are becoming like a cancer to our world, and so our anthropogenic environment in turn becomes carcinogenic to us.

Hence, we dispel some fundamental dogmas about what drives human behavior. Our intention and beliefs interact with our biology and behavior. As our business environment undergoes significant transformation, it will be ever more important for individuals (as well as organizations) to be able to adapt to change successfully.

As explored in *Presence*, the excellent book by Peter M. Senge, C. Otto Scharmer, Joseph Jaworski and Betty Sue Flowers, our senses do not actually perceive the world; rather, they participate in the world. In *Presence*, Greg Merten, general manager of Hewlett-Packard's inkjet suppliers' operations, explored this in relation to business leadership:

> We see the world not as it is but as we are... If I want to see things change out there, first I need to see change in here... At the heart of the challenge facing HP — and lots of other businesses — is the

way information moves around the world... When Humberto says that "love is the only emotion that expands intelligence," it reminds us that legitimacy and trust are crucial for the free flow of information and how information gets transformed into value. We will need to use the heart more, which means the quality of our being and relationships with one another become more and more central in allowing an organization to flourish.[4]

The organization and community

We have 50 trillion cells working cooperatively within our bodies. They come together to act as one body. We find millions of organisms living in cooperation within a handful of healthy soil, a thriving ecosystem from which life can flourish. While our consumption rates exponentially increase and our population shoots beyond seven billion, we find ourselves exploiting our lands, our seas, our air, our own people and our home at a rate that is undermining our very existence. We are now perhaps entering the sixth mass extinction of life on Earth, and the first to be solely caused by one species: us.

In our pursuit of happiness, we have tried to control life and force predictability into business. Predictability stifles creativity and inhibits learning and growth. As explored earlier, diverse, interconnected, open, emergent organizations may appear more chaotic and difficult to manage, yet they are vibrant places for people to be self-empowered, inspiring others around them — self-learning and self-managing through mutual understanding of correct behaviors rooted in core values and clarity of purpose.

It is this shared value set that ensures the chaotic nature of diversity aligns toward the overall value-creation goals of the organization. The collection of people within the organization becomes a stakeholder community. The community needs the values of the organizational culture to bind it together while bridging it to partner organizations in its wider business ecosystem; setting the diverse set of stakeholders free to interact, self-govern and be creative rather than limiting and controlling community behavior in some way. Just as important to the vitality of the community is the value-creation mission of the organization, which provides the community identity. For the community to be authentic and lasting, the values and value purpose must come from within, not be imposed through an organizational hierarchy but emerging through community awareness of how best to sense, adapt and respond to the environment in order to deliver right value with right values.[5]

> The key is, in some measure, to let the company go and to allow it to be managed by the community that defines it, to allow it to evolve into what they desire it to be. From the collective actions of its executives, employees, customers, and other stakeholders, something new will emerge. The company will be a product of their mutual creation.
> — TACHI KIUCHI AND BILL SHIREMAN[6]

A lot of research and experience has already been undertaken on how organizations can become more organic, adaptive and responsive. For example, the need for organizations to break down barriers between departments and be structured around teams that are responsible for the whole process from design to delivery is recommended in W. Edwards Deming's seminal *Out of the Crisis*.[7] This idea is central to business process reengineering (as promoted by Michael Hammer), to Morgan's six models of organization, to Morgan's holographic organization and to lean management, as observed with some of the most successful Japanese manufacturers.[8] In these organizations, capabilities are distributed and teams aim to be cross-functional, with people being broadly trained rather than specialized so that they are interchangeable, and equipment being more general purpose and organized in cells that produce a group of similar products rather than specialized by process stage.[9]

Peter Senge explores the learning organization in his visionary book *The Fifth Discipline*.[10] He explores how organizations need to become more akin to learning living organisms, where leaders teach, coach and empower others, inspiring through a sense of purpose. The learning organization needs to encourage creativity and emergence within its organizational culture. According to Ed Simon, former President and

COO of Herman Miller, "only when it is vision-led will an organization embrace change...the learning cycle is a continuous process of experimentation. You cannot experiment without taking risks."[11]

The learning organization is where ideas are encouraged and mistakes are viewed as lessons to be learned along the way. Unfortunately, the prevailing organizational cultural paradigm is more about risk aversion, where mistakes are to be avoided at all costs, leading to a cultural fear of experimentation, in turn reducing learning and strategic resilience. The firm of the future is a shift in mindset for leaders and employees alike toward "generative learning" among diverse work groups.

It is the diversity and increased propensity for experimentation that offsets and mitigates any cost or perceived loss incurred through mistakes. "Tata wants its people to be able to act without always having to receive direct orders," says Satish Pradhan, Chief Group Human Resources at Tata Sons. "We are not here to make decisions for people," he says. "Our role is to help people become better able to make the right decisions. We don't want credit for what they do. We want them to be able to say, 'We did this ourselves.'"[12]

Again, we witness another of life's paradoxes: focus and control with diversity and freedom. Finding the right harmonic within this paradox (which may vary depending on the circumstances at hand) is how optimal positive adaptation is best found. Dee Hock (founder of VISA), in seeking how best to design his business, devised a concept called "chaordic organizations."[13] Chaordic organizations are always on the border between order and chaos, providing malleability and durability. According to Hock, "The organization of the future will be an embodiment of community based on shared purpose calling on the higher aspirations of people."[14]

Leadership of the future

Leaders of the future unleash human potential with clarity of purpose and an openness to continual learning aligned with core values. Leaders are the learners, the ones who seek "personal mastery" (as Peter Senge puts it) while remaining interconnected to the whole. Leaders are people who understand who they really are, aspire toward greatness in themselves and inspire greatness in others (not egotistic greatness but soulful greatness). Leaders become teachers, taking time to assist and empower others to lead themselves. The quest for optimal leadership is about encouraging a creative tension — balancing personal mastery with openness and a deep sense of belonging among a community of stakeholders across a diverse business ecosystem. Jamsetji N. Tata, founder of Tata Group, has noted that, in a free enterprise, "the community is not just another stakeholder in our businesses but is in fact the very purpose of their existence."[15]

This is another of life's nuances — finding the harmonics of the individual and the collective learning, where each is symbiotic with the other. This collective–individual harmony may challenge the current prevailing view of individualism, yet it is a natural evolution from it. While it is imperative to have a wholesome, ambitious view of oneself, this self-improvement strategy goes hand in hand with a sense of interconnectedness, belongingness, co-creativity and sharing that comes with community (organizational and societal). The organization's value set, vision and culture encourage self-inspiration and empowerment, while encouraging interconnectedness. Only then does the need to manage, monitor and control the stakeholders fall away, its cumbersome governance mechanism of hierarchic management being replaced by good governance through values and walking-the-talk behaviors, where people embody the change they wish to see.

Andy Wood, CEO of Adnams, believes that "the job of a leader is to sprinkle water on to talent and allow it to grow."[16] Create the conditions conducive to co-creation, and it will naturally flourish. Virtuous cycles start to unlock as people find the optimal pathways for their own value-creation potential, with the desire to overcome challenges, learn, help and share experiences feeding it. Less energy is siphoned from value-creation activities to management overhead, leaving more available to move forward with the vision of the organization and innovate. Self-empowerment and collective orientation overcome challenges with opportunities; the leaders refocus their attention from management to empowerment — encouragement through coaching, rather than management through fear.

Emergent leadership (as referred to by Fritjof Capra) encourages an environment of continual questioning and new approaches to problems.[17] This culture of emergence needs to spread beyond the organization to the stakeholder community, hence encouraging emergence across the business ecosystem, improving resilience of the whole and the parts.

> Ricardo Semler, CEO of Semco, presents himself as "the questioner," "the challenger" and "the catalyst": as the person who asked basic questions and encouraged people to bring things down to the simplest level in making key decisions shaping their work performance. By challenging the status quo at every turn and allowing people to come up with appropriate solutions, the attack on bureaucracy and conventional styles of management became more and more dramatic, leading to many novel innovations... His particular skill and genius has been to recognize the self-organizing potentials that were unleashed and how he could build a new organization around them, meeting forks in the road as they arose and nudging the organization along an appropriate path.[18]

Increasingly, as the organization is required to become more emergent, so leadership is more about empowering, empathizing and encouraging interconnections, innovation, local attunement and an active network of feedback. As organizations and business ecosystems become more self-organizing and self-empowering, the working environment and culture becomes more emotionally and mentally healthy, where business goals are met without sacrificing personal values and integrity. Quite the contrary, in fact: work acts to reinforce personal integrity in providing a rich emergent experience for individual and collective learning and ethical growth.

The more our working environments become life-enhancing, the more alive the organizations and the more aligned we become to the true nature within us and around us. A growing number of business leaders recognize this, including many of those already encountered in these pages: Paul Polman of Unilever, Mark Parker of Nike, Richard

Leadership of the future characteristics
- networked
- bottom-up
- empowering
- emergent
- inspiring
- values-led
- quality and relationship-oriented
- encouraging diversity, innovation and collaboration
- opportunity-driven
- courage-based.

Branson of Virgin, Andy Wood of Adnams, Ricardo Semler of Semco, to name a few.

Leadership of the future is less about the theory of an idealized leadership model and more about the practical ability to navigate a journey of authenticity and inspiration, thus energizing and equipping oneself and others to make the right choices for the situation at hand.

Complex, self-organizing, emergent firms of the future recognize that change emerges in unpredictable ways, and that overarching bureaucratic mechanisms no longer assist emergent organizational evolution. The role of leadership is to actively participate in enabling and facilitating local change, by encouraging effective communications through clarity of understanding of how to behave, act and interact. Each and every one of us plays our part in leadership of the future by helping others to co-create toward positive outcomes. Each day challenges us to walk the talk; each day offers us opportunities to learn, grow and evolve.

While we each may need leadership to inspire us and give us courage, especially in volatile times, we each have a unique blend of talents. It is up to us to unlock our creative potential, to utilize our talents to our best endeavors, and it is also up to us to help others to unlock their creative potential in their time of need, and in so doing helping them help themselves and others. The more we open up to our environment, the more we tune in to the interconnected nature of business life, sensing and responding in the most optimal way.

Becoming aware of the whole (social, economic and environmental) value-creation potential and impact of the organization helps flush out misunderstandings among stakeholders. This is where integrated reporting (social, economic and environmental) can greatly help the understanding and awareness of all stakeholders. This depth of understanding and clarity of purpose can only fully emerge through open dialogue between diverse stakeholder communities, who are empowered and encouraged to share their locally attuned experiences. Metaphorically, the organization becomes more akin to a fungal network beneath the forest floor, constantly exploring and feeding back information across its network, expanding in some areas, assimilating in others, and conserving or declining in yet others — all aspects of the cycle of life accommodated, each interrelated to the other, sharing experiences and findings, making the diverse stakeholder community of the whole strategically resilient, adaptive and optimal in its value-creation potential, while mitigating negative impacts.

Stakeholder empowerment

There is a shift emerging in human resources → employee engagement → stakeholder empowerment. Here is a guiding approach to stakeholder empowerment. The firm of the future is one that:

1. Facilitates collaboration between diverse stakeholders.
2. Empowers stakeholders to influence the local direction of the business, through open dialogue, sharing and trust.
3. Encourages leadership that is values-led, adaptive and locally attuned.
4. Attracts a talented, motivated, high-performing, diverse stakeholder community, which embodies the ideals and ethics of the organization and wider ecosystem.
5. Motivates stakeholders through feedback relationships at a local level.
6. Ensures proactive decision-making, where mistakes are viewed

as learning and feedback communication is clear, simple and effective.

As complexities of our global, digitized working environments increase, so too can the potential for remoteness or "disconnectedness" from each other as employees and stakeholders (e.g., from the organization and its end customers). Fast-moving-consumer-goods (FMCG) organizations of today, for example, are trying to reconnect their employees and decision-makers with the "real consumers" to help encourage feedback on what the real experiences, needs and values of their customer base are.

As organizations have become more hierarchical and complex, they have also become more reliant on intermediaries or third parties to inform on feedback sensations, experiences and emotions from the environment which the organization is serving. These intermediaries and niche partners play an important role in value creation providing specialist local insight and niche expertise, yet they can also encourage a distancing of the organization from directly experiencing its customer base and environment within which it operates. It is important for the organization to enhance its own sensory perception of the environment it operates in (supplier, investor, partner and customer environment alike), while also calling on niche local partners to aid specific value-enhancement initiatives.

Being in touch with and empathizing with the stakeholder environment is one activity that is foolish to outsource completely. There are lots of exciting initiatives going on at present with organizations of all sizes directly connecting with all aspects of their customer base. For example, Danone uses local charity organizations to engage its employees and partners with customers all over the world, immersing them in customer everyday life. This could mean staying for a week with a family in less economically developed areas of the world so that each can relate to each other, encouraging co-creativity and understanding between stakeholder groups.[19]

The increased awareness of the effect the organization has on the other stakeholders within the community brings greater realization of the sense of community. This helps reinforce business behavior, which upholds the welfare of the wider ecosystem.

The conscious company[20]

The more the conscious behavior of the people working for an organization aligns with the values and culture of that organization, the more conscious the organization becomes — the individuals benefiting the whole and the whole benefiting the individuals, and so conscious awareness increases for each and all with good business sense prevailing. In the words of Alfred Schmits, who heads up a consultancy based in The Netherlands called The Conscious Company:

> You are not working in a Conscious Company, you are living it. A conscious goal in the heart and mind is more powerful for the motivation of the workforce than a business goal in the mind alone. And the workforce produces the profit.

For a conscious company, effective communication among stakeholders is important; this ensures that the best proposition for the customer is continually sought. Today, the vast majority of organizational hierarchy charts do not include customers. There are sales and marketing departments who define customers in terms of abstractions of the real thing. The customers are seen as outside the company. In a conscious company, guidelines and shared values are more important than hierarchy or structure. Everyone is free to create customer intimacy with responsibility being anchored in trustworthiness, self-reflection and professionalism.

Since a conscious company does not have a hierarchical management structure but a value system, it is important that stakeholders and employees regularly connect with each other on an emotional and intellectual level. A conscious company is a people's business based on trust, and while social media can help facilitate communications, the organization cannot run on virtual communications alone. Social media and collaboration technologies help emergent interaction enormously, but emotions are best shared in person (or at least via phone, Skype or telepresence).

A conscious company is not always a peaceful company, since everything happens in the transparency of conscious interactions; everybody participating in such a conscious community does so out of free choice and is free to leave if she or he is not synchronizing with the development and direction of the community or the individuals in it. Participation is a synergy of delivering organizational value and gaining personal value. In a way, nobody is depending on the conscious company and everybody is contributing to it by being wholeheartedly involved. This can seem daunting to manage for the old-school top-down manager, whereas it can be liberating and stimulating for emergent, creative leaders and participants of the conscious company. In practice, people who understand networking, togetherness, integrity and trustworthiness are people who often adhere to values-led systems embedded with sustainability. In this way, conscious companies are by nature on their way to becoming firms of the future.

> In the long history of good and trying times, Tata founders have viewed business from a higher level of consciousness and purpose. Beyond creating high-quality products and services, they have demonstrated immense and real care for people, human well-being and the ecosystems which sustain all of us. The "blueprint" was deeply engraved in the minds, hearts and institutional memory of all those who dealt with or served our enterprises; and all Tata leaders and group chairmen faithfully and relentlessly created that kind of thought and action space to run our businesses. In this "ether" of consistent leadership and business practice our journey is so precious, special and eternal.
> — MANISH VAIDYA[21]

> You cannot keep earning profits indefinitely at the expense of the people who work for you or live near you, or of your customers or your suppliers. When it comes to sustainable enterprise, it really is all or nothing, and we are all in it together.
> — RAY ANDERSON[22]

Learning from indigenous people [23]

While it is important not to fall into slipshod romanticism about the lives and lifestyles of indigenous peoples, it is impossible to refute the fact that people who live in close proximity to nature, and rely on the biophysical systems of nature for their survival, have a highly complex and developed relationship with their environment. Indigenous people have learned through bitter experience that you cannot just take from nature in an over-exploitative manner; you have to build a nurturing relationship with that which sustains life. This relationship need not be one solely of reverence; it can also be one of utilization, but utilization based on essential needs rather than endless wants. Unlike the exploitation which underpins the prevailing business paradigm, "indigenous utilization" has a combination of spiritual, pragmatic and practical elements that respect natural limits and can teach the firm of the future so much.

Indigenous utilization has allowed people to survive in some of Earth's most inhospitable environments for many thousands of years. The Aboriginal peoples of Australia, for example, survived and flourished for thousands of years on one of Earth's driest continents — until, of course, they were colonized. By learning to adapt to extreme environmental conditions, Aboriginal Australians built cultures that were adapted to their environments. This adaptation, based on highly efficient resource utilization, allowed Aboriginal people to build thriving cultures in environments where even the most technologically advanced "Westerners" struggle to survive.

By looking at how indigenous people relate to their environments and how they use resources, the firm of the future can learn how best to adapt to the volatile conditions ahead. Importantly, the value systems of indigenous people can also inform the firm of the future. Reciprocity, for example, allows balance in indigenous communities, and it is balance that underpins resilience. Reciprocity also underpins the respectful relationship that many indigenous people had, and have, with nature. You don't simply steal from nature; you care for it so that it will care for you.

Interestingly, "sustainability" as a term does not really exist among indigenous cultures simply because indigenous people live it (not think about it in a separate way to normal behavior). This is why they have thrived for thousands of years in volatile environments and lived to tell the tale. By embodying the notion of right relationships, reciprocity, reverence, thinking generations ahead while having a holistic understanding of their natural and social environment, they ensure their actions form part of the interconnected nature of life. Hence, sustainability is not needed as a concept as it would never occur to them not to behave and live in a sustainable way.

Creative thinking[24]

Each human is born with an immense creative potential. Conventional mentality, schools of thought and belief dogmas have pervaded our education and upbringing. Reductionist approaches to life are encouraged through left-brain analytical thinking at school, at work and in society, often inadequately balanced by right-brain creativity, empathy and interconnectedness. We have been, and continue to be, conditioned by prevalent paradigms that permeate our beliefs and thoughts, in turn affecting our creative potential.

"Creative thinking" brings much-needed tools and techniques to organizations and individuals in order to encourage our innate creative potential so the creativity and the analysis can interweave hand in hand. It is, after all, creativity that spawns new thought that is so very important in the firm of the future. So let's explore what "creative thinking" is and how we can encourage it.

Thinking underlies almost everything we do. It has become popular to add the adjective "creative" to "thinking" to indicate a different kind of thinking. Although there is a sense in which thinking is itself a creative act, creative thinking has come to represent a kind of thinking that breaks existing patterns and produces new ideas.

Traditionally, this has been seen as the province of artists and other "creatives." However, artists or not, we are born with brains capable of enormous creativity. What lies between our ears is a vital natural resource with almost unlimited capacity. It needs to be prioritized for development. So, how might a firm of the future promote creative thinking?

Time to think

There seems to be little free space in today's world. Rather, there is a continual invitation (some might call it pressure) to do "more" at work and away from work. In-between, the little gaps, transition times, waiting times and travelling times become filled with sounds and pictures, accompanied with the ever-present handheld device. It is as though we have become unable to tolerate space, quiet, not doing — the very things which are so essential to creative thinking.[25]

So how can you make more time to think?

* **Restore some of the in-between times.** Experiment with not filling in every available moment — the brain needs "idling time." For example, if you have a journey to work by bus or train, try one day a week without access to phone, iPod, newspaper or book, etc.
* **Spend some quiet time in nature** — by water, in the woods, in the countryside. Besides refreshing your physical self, the stimulation of the natural world coupled with quiet nourishes the mind.
* **Protect "thinking time" at work** by identifying it and giving it separate time. Bill Gates used to (and maybe still does) take whole weeks away from the workplace just to focus on new ideas and new thinking. Others work on a smaller scale. A successful theater director used to dedicate Friday morning each week for this. Four hours for four subjects that needed thought. It was in her calendar, and her staff learned not to disturb her then. Some people prefer to go away from the workplace to have productive thinking time. There are many to choose from — including cafés, hot desks, motorway service station workplaces, a park bench. A good way to get started is to put appointments with yourself in your calendar, boundaries to protect your thinking time.
* **Be a model for others.** Leaders set the model within organizations for what is permissible behavior. If a leader is seen to value thinking time, it can give others permission to do the same.

Improving thinking skills

Creative thinking as a subject has been largely ignored in formal education. However, it can be taught and learned. There are many writers and teachers who can provide practical tools and steps to get started. Just put "creative thinking" or "creative thinking tools" into a search engine to get lots of responses.

Two experienced and powerful writers and teachers are Edward de Bono and Tony Buzan. They have both written many books that offer practical ways of accessing one's creative thought processes to produce new responses to a problem, new ways of thinking about possibilities. De Bono's *The Thinking Course* and Buzan's *How to Mind Map* would be good places to start.[26] They both have or are connected to organizations that provide training in their methods.

Thinking together

New ideas in an organization are rarely produced in isolation. One person's brain may have trillions of possible idea permutations, but that brain working with others has this amount many times over. This is partly due to sheer numbers of neurons at work and also due to the power of our own thought patterns interacting with others. A familiar thought pattern will be a more likely thought path than a new one. Other people's perspectives and ideas can open up whole new patterns that would previously have been invisible.

The challenge is that although thinking together is a key element in effective creative thinking, like thinking itself, it is rarely taught directly. Thinking together successfully uses the skills of listening, communicating, facilitating and collaborating. Observe people who display these abilities. If they are lacking where you work, bring in people with these skills to demonstrate and share them. Look for opportunities to practice — opportunities to think together with others. Keith Sawyer's book *Group Genius* is full of practical principles and examples at work.[27]

Develop a "creative thinking" culture within the organization

There is just so much that you can do on your own. It is also vital to be working to develop the organization's own environment in order to encourage a culture in which creative thinking is nurtured and encouraged. Though culture is a complex subject, the following actions can all make positive contributions:

- **Be a role model.** Leaders are carefully watched for signs of behavior that is appropriate or inappropriate. For creative thinking and the risk-taking that accompanies it to be seen as OK, formal and informal leaders need to be models of what is desired.

- **Spread the good word** — whether in the form of direct appreciation or "positive gossip." We all respond to encouragement and recognition. Research has also shown that creativity is more likely to flourish in an environment where people are appreciated and their work is recognized. "Change the gossip and you change the organization."[28]

- **Build supportive structures.** Google's "20% time" for engineers and W. L. Gore's half day a week of "dabble time" are institutional ways of giving a clear signal about what is permitted and rewarded. Reward people for coming with new ideas and getting them tested. Change the appraisal and review processes. People will take notice when promotion starts depending on people's ability to think creatively and encouraging others to do so.

- **Improve the physical environment.** The story is told that when he was thinking about a cure for polio, Dr. Jonas Salk travelled to Assisi in Italy to clear his head. He spent time among the columns and cloistered courtyards of a thirteenth-century monastery and was convinced that the setting was responsible for all the ideas he had, including the vital breakthrough. As a result, he contracted architect Louis Kahn to build the Salk Institute in La Jolla, California — as a scientific facility to stimulate breakthroughs and creativity.[29]

Different workplaces have different effects on people working within them. Space, height, light, air, sound, layout will all impact on the physical experience of being there. Changing the environment can change the experience.

An enriched physical workplace enhances creativity by providing accessible, casual meeting spots; physical stimuli; space for quiet reflection; a variety of communication tools, e.g., white boards,

bulletin boards; contact space for clients, audiences, and partners; and room for individual expression, among others.
— OLIVIER SERRAT[30]

The best conditions for thinking, if you really stop and notice, are not tense. They are gentle. They are quiet. They are unrushed. They are stimulating but not competitive. They are encouraging. They are paradoxically both rigorous and nimble.
— NANCY KLINE[31]

Getting started

Solution-focused approaches and experiential learning techniques (such as embodied learning, improvization and role-playing) build on the concept of emergence discussed earlier.[32] In finding solutions, people need to just start sharing ideas and get going. Even if the first tentative steps may not be perfectly placed (they seldom are), just getting started and having the confidence to commence the transformation (no matter how small or big and daunting) is where it all begins. By looking at what can work and going with that, the motion forward toward possible solutions is commenced.

Beyond these first tentative steps, scenario planning and iterative planning approaches can aid navigation for the transformation ahead. These approaches are gaining popularity over rigid business plans which often become restrictive and limiting in an unpredictable business environment.

> The ritual of predict, plan and implement may allay anxiety about the future, but it is a crummy way to advance into an unknowable future. A linear approach forces planners to lock into a mental map without benefit of information that will emerge in the future.
> — DONALD SULL[33]

Scenario-planning can flush out possible future break points, disruptions (positive or negative) and trajectories (with qualitative and quantitative assumptions built in). Iterative revisiting and gauging of these scenarios as events unfold ensure stakeholders and decision-makers understand the wider holistic picture (the social, economic and environmental interconnections) and the local impacts with their specific cause-and-effect decisions.

In the next module, we explore ways to enhance the transformational process through "catalysts for transformation."

Tips for Transformation: The Seven S's

1. **Silence** — A quiet mind helps ensure a successful outcome. Be still and allow the mind to quieten as often as possible throughout the day. From silence the mind is more able to identify the right choices for the road ahead.
2. **Sense** — Be in the moment. Learn to really "listen" to yourself and others. The local environment provides vital feedback, "feel" this feedback, tune in and act/adapt accordingly.
3. **Strategy** — Ensure clarity of direction for the meandering path ahead. What are your instincts saying? What really turns you on? What makes your heart sing? Why are you doing what you are doing? Follow your heart with a clear mind. Allow it to navigate your transformation with passion and conviction.
4. **Small steps** — Each step provides chances to make positive change happen. Endeavor to take each step, each interaction and intervention with authenticity.
5. **Stakeholders** — Recognize, engage and empower the interested parties. Tensions may be uncomfortable and energy/time-consuming, yet they are inevitable and can help hone right navigation for the path ahead. Through stakeholder engagement, tension can become a constructive force stimulating learning and development; where "dinergy" leads to synergy.
6. **Systems** — Transcend perceived boundaries to see connectedness; the interconnected systems of relationships and resources.
7. **Solutions** — Problems and challenges abound, and the glass can often seem half-empty in challenging times. Explore solutions, the art of the possible; what can be done (rather than what cannot) through solution-creating, collaborating, prototyping and experimenting. Channel energy from fear and worry to the exploration of solutions.

Questions

1. If on your way to work tomorrow you died in an accident, what would your colleagues say about you — the good qualities and the not-so-good qualities? What would you like your colleagues to say about you?

2. If you did die tomorrow, would you have any regrets? If so, what are they?

3. Do you ever look back over the last year and gain perspective on your perceived success? How do you gauge your personal success?

4. How do you value your work? Is it through quantities of things and/or qualities of feelings?

5. List three of your most successful accomplishments in work to date. What do you value about these accomplishments at a personal level?

6. List the three things you like most about your job (or current activity) and the three things you like least.

7. If you could change one thing about your work, what would it be? Think about why you would change this one thing and how you would go about changing it.

8. Would you describe yourself as a person with strong values? If so, what are those values?

9. Are you motivated away from something (pain) and/or toward something (goal)?

10. How do you like to be treated by other people in business? Is that how you treat others regardless of status or role?

11. How important to you is your position within the organizational hierarchy? Why?

12. What could you change in your current work environment to encourage creative thinking?

13. Are there any customers, colleagues and suppliers that you really enjoy working with? Why them? What is it about the relationship that you enjoy?

14. Would you describe yourself as a leader? If you had to lead a group of people through a period of significant turbulence, how would you go about it? What qualities would it ask of you?

15. Which managers in your working career have you been grateful for? What did you learn or gain from their management style or leadership approach? What made them good managers or leaders in your eyes?

16. Imagine a time in your personal life when you let go, perhaps of a plan or goal or "your way," and things turned out surprisingly well, even

better than expected. How might you foster letting go in your business to achieve better-than-planned-for results?

17. How would you describe your organization's strategy? Is the intent or purpose clear to everyone? Is management more about "command and control" or "inspire and support"? Are there values along with the objectives?

18. How locally attuned, feedback-oriented and empowering is your organization? How would you go about encouraging a more locally attuned, feedback-oriented and empowering business environment?

Catalysts for Transformation

> Vision without action is merely
> a dream. Action without vision
> just passes the time. Vision with
> action can change the world.
>
> — Joel A. Barker

EXECUTIVE SUMMARY

:- There are four primary catalysts for transformation: collaboration, innovation, education and inspiration.
:- Collaboration through business relations built on mutual trust.
:- Innovation through creativity and courage to do things differently.
:- Education through values and culture that walk the talk.
:- Inspiration through case studies and sharing what good looks like.

Make no mistake, the transformation from a firm of the past to a firm of the future is challenging, especially while operating amid immense volatility. Successful transformation requires courage, not fear; it is not for the faint-hearted. The more we understand and explore our own business environments and wider business ecosystems (as well as our own inner motives and values), the more we find pathways for success — learning through doing, growth through experience, success through failure. Looking around us in nature and human nature, we find enablers to assist us — catalysts that aid and optimize the transformational journey. Let's explore each of the four primary catalysts for transformation in turn.

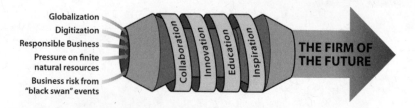

Figure 9. Catalysts for transformation.

Collaboration

There has been much written recently about collaboration and cooperation. In fact, this decade (2010–2020) has been referred to as the decade
of cooperation, a time when business executives recognize the power of
collaboration and cooperation over competition. As explored earlier, it
is a myth that nature has evolved over millions of years of combat and
competitive struggle; its evolution is more down to networking and
partnerships. Of course there has been competition in life, and there
always will be, yet life's evolution benefits far more from collaboration
than it does from competition. It is the same in our business environment, present and future. We are witnessing a shift in mentality and
behavior from the firm-of-the-past approach of dog-eat-dog competition between businesses, business units, and employees to the firm-of-
the-future approach of collaboration across multifunctional teams, departments, organizations and business ecosystems: interconnectedness
rather than separateness, collaboration rather than competition.

Collaboration interconnects artificial separations in business, encouraging sharing, creativity, empowerment and innovation. The more
we recognize the interconnectedness of the business environment —
viewing it as a web of interdependent relationships within interconnected business ecosystems — the more we realize that collaboration
(not competition) is key to our resilience in these volatile times.

In nature, with its 3.8 billion years of learning, we find that it is the
species that collaborate and interconnect more with their respective
ecosystems that are more resilient to changes in their environment; the
ecosystem they live in becomes more resilient the more interconnected
the stakeholders are within that ecosystem — ditto for business.

> Cooperation is the architect of creativity throughout evolution, from cells to multicellular creatures to anthills to villages to cities. Without cooperation there can be neither construction nor complexity in evolution.
>
> — Nowak and Highfield[1]

An example to illustrate this shift in business mentality is the evolution of supply-chain management → value chain management → business ecosystem resilience. Rather than treating an organization as a supplier that needs managing and controlling, we treat the organization as a partner within an ecosystem where synergies are created that benefit the whole as well as the parts. Rather than viewing supplier management as a linear chain, we view it as a web of interconnected relationships within a vibrant business ecosystem.

Another example to illustrate this shift is the evolution in approach of human resource management → employee engagement → stakeholder empowerment we spoke of earlier. Rather than treating the employee as an asset to be managed and controlled, we treat the employee as a stakeholder within a community of diverse, interdependent stakeholders empowered to create synergies through mutually beneficial relationships with other stakeholders. Such collaboration between stakeholders significantly improves creativity, enabling sharing between people with differing perspectives on a problem. This helps embed a culture more open to dynamic change.

It is the openness of connections across, within and beyond the organization that drives the opportunities for value enhancement while building strategic resilience from the ground up for the organization and the business ecosystem within which it thrives. If any stakeholder seeks to undercut, exploit or compete in some way, the value of the relationship is undermined, in turn reducing the opportunity for synergies and the resilience of the business ecosystem and so the resilience of the contributing stakeholders within that ecosystem. Of course, such collaboration requires trust, mutual understanding and shared values. Trust is both "the glue and the lubricant that allow us to collaborate."[2] Collaboration itself helps foster trust rather than tension, mutualism rather than parasitism, and cooperation rather than competition.

The more collaborative interconnectedness in a firm of the future and its business ecosystem, the more sharing and synergies, hence the more chance for virtuous cycles of empowered new ways of working to take root and thrive.

Innovation

Increased market volatility brings with it the need to create, develop and adapt new products and services under time-pressured conditions. Hence, the ability to innovate is a critical success factor for the firm of the future — organizations able to innovate effectively, time and again, shall succeed while others struggle to adapt. Innovation is fundamental to evolution in all walks of life, not just in business, but for all living species experiencing the need to change in times of challenge.

Ecover (a medium-sized consumer goods company) fosters collaboration with suppliers and customers wherever possible. In seeking to minimize waste in its products' life cycles, it works collaboratively with suppliers to co-create new approaches in package design and recycling, ensuring the reuse of packaging where possible. This also benefits the supplier. Some of Ecover's suppliers have sought to implement this new packaging-recycling approach with other manufacturers (which could be viewed as competitors of Ecover). This enhances the resilience of the suppliers by differentiating them from others while strengthening their relations with their customers (manufacturers), in turn building resilience into Ecover's supplier base. It also ensures Ecover's business values of minimizing environmental impact where possible are extended beyond its own immediate business ecosystem. Ecover also engages collaboratively with customers through social media. It asks customers to vote on possible ingredients and fragrances for its products. This not only leads to enhanced product value but also encourages co-creation, and so shared buy-in with the customer community, which again enhances resilience through improved customer loyalty.

The good news is that humans are opportunistic and curious by nature; it is in our genes to seek out new and better ways of operating. The firm of the future creates the conditions conducive to creativity by building a culture that facilitates, empowers, unlocks and supports people's creative potential; an organization which encourages people to overcome fears and inhibitions, where the work dynamic is of constant evolution, where failure is not criticized but embraced for what it is — an opportunity to learn, adapt and evolve. Innovative organizational cultures thrive in unpredictability, ambiguity and novelty — not stability, bureaucracy and certainty.

> Google and Apple maintain entrepreneurial and innovative cultures by forming small teams that act like individual start-ups, while encouraging creative thinking, openness, and the sharing of new ideas.

Of course, collaboration greatly helps innovation by sharing the burden of innovation on a wider group of stakeholders. As organisms evolve best in nature within diverse groups of interconnected species, so does an organization's ability to innovate and improve with collaboration among diverse stakeholder groups. For example, it is becoming more commonplace for multinationals to partner (or joint venture) with niche start-ups to gain their innovative edge. One instance of this is PepsiCo10 — a group of UK and European technology start-ups that will be receiving financial help in return for working with PepsiCo on "innovative marketing."[3]

> Cisco balances acquisitions (tending to focus on smaller more innovative players) with a diverse partner ecosystem (ensuring a richness of external stimuli) and high R&D spending (to germinate good ideas), ensuring it continually innovates in a fast-evolving marketplace.

"Open innovation" describes the interaction of both internal and external sources to create innovation and is emerging as a powerful tool for transformation. Open innovation goes hand in hand with collaboration across a diverse stakeholder community. It treats R&D as an open, collaborative system. Crowd-sourcing and co-creation are also forms of open innovation where the public (or a large selected group of contributors) share ideas to co-create innovative solutions to problems. Innovation consultancy OVO describe it as follows:

> Open innovation is the use of purposive inflows and outflows of knowledge to accelerate internal innovation, and expand the markets for external use of innovation, respectively.[4]

Traditionally, businesses have tended to apply the concept of an "innovation funnel," where creative ideas are transformed along the funnel by individuals and teams within the company into successful business outcomes. An evolution of this by Henry Chesbrough is the "open innovation funnel." With open innovation, Chesbrough argues that ideas ought to come not just from internal individuals and teams but also from external customers and partners. Hence, the funnel is permeable and porous; ideas from within the company are collaboratively enriched with the help of partners and clients.[5]

Innovation Exchange (IX) is an online open innovation marketplace. It's where diverse community members from all over the world respond to challenges sponsored by Global 5000 companies and not-for-profit organizations.[6]

Jovoto is a co-creation platform that connects organizations with designers and innovators around the globe. It helps organizations gain access to a wide, diverse set of creative minds while providing opportunities for creative people (particularly those just starting out) to earn money, learn and build their reputations.[7]

Education

Embracing new approaches to ways of operating is facilitated through an understanding and trust in what, why and how change affects the stakeholders and their respective communities. Ensuring all stakeholder communities are engaged, aware and educated in the transformational journey of the firm of the future greatly optimizes the transformative process. The deeper the understanding, the greater the sense of belonging to the transformation — not just being aware of the changes coming, but really empathizing with what it means, why it is happening and how it affects the ecosystem of stakeholders involved.

This deeper understanding not only helps the transformation within the department or wider organization, but also across the interconnected network of stakeholders that the organization is part of — its business ecosystem. We are all being exposed to increased volatility — our suppliers, associates, investors, shareholders, regulators, unions, employees, customers and so on. By educating individuals to a level of deep understanding of the values and direction of the transformational journey, these individuals become proponents for change; they are able to educate other stakeholders they interact with as part of their daily business. The understanding of the transformation, the why and how of it, becomes viral if it is grounded in trust and truth. Hence, the values of the organization need to deeply resonate with the stakeholders, to strike a chord of belief beyond the goal of short-term profit maximization.

Keeping stakeholders in the dark or partially aware will only come back to haunt those that try it, and in turn this will water down the effectiveness of the transformational journey. This does not mean to say that complete clarity of where the organization will be in one or two years from now is needed; it is more that people truly understand the reasons for change, the drivers for transformation and the value set of the organization, and so they understand the general direction it is taking to navigate these volatile times. The transformation is more about the journey than the destination, with plots on the course helping to steer a course through choppy water, while being flexible to changes in wind and tide. A firm of the future has a culture that is rooted in values and where the awareness of right and wrong behavior is second nature. Organizations that encourage the right mentality, by living and breathing their values, ensure that openness, awareness, acceptance and motivation for transformation follow.

More education can help us only if it produces more wisdom.
The essence of education, I suggest, is the transmission of values,
but values do not help us to pick our way through life unless they
have become our own, a part, so to say, of our mental make-up.
— E. F. Schumacher[8]

Inspiration

We are entering uncharted waters. We are on the cusp of major transformative change socially, economically and environmentally. Few business leaders have witnessed volatility of the likes we are now faced with.
Inspiration is what provides us with the ability to explore uncharted
waters. Inspiration can come from any and all of us — whether it is a visionary CEO committing to zero-emissions by 2020, a new sustainable
product line being launched to much success, a neighboring plant successfully implementing new sustainable processes, or a colleague taking
time out from a pressing schedule to brainstorm with another in a time
of need.

> Inspiration is not garnered from litanies of what is flawed; it
> resides in humanity's willingness to restore, redress, reform, re-
> cover, reimagine and reconsider.
> — Paul Hawken[9]

We do not have to be inspired by visionaries or great leaders. In these
transformational times, we need to inspire ourselves and the ones
around us by simply walking the talk and being true to the values of
the organizations and communities we serve. The culture of the firm of
the future encourages inspiration through the sharing of inspirational
stories and case studies from within and outside the organization — the
more we look for examples of inspiration within our own business ecosystems, the more we find, and in turn the more it will inspire ourselves
to be the change we wish to see.

Questions

Collaboration

1. Do you see yourself as a collaborator? When was the last time you offered to share openly with a colleague or partner organization? How did you find that experience?

2. Is there an embedded sense of sharing among your colleagues? How could it be improved upon?

3. Can you think of or find examples of similar organizations that collaborate effectively within their business ecosystem?

4. How often does your organization ask other partner/supplier/customer organizations to come together in one place and share experiences, challenges and opportunities?

Innovation

1. Do you see yourself as innovative? When was the last time you personally innovated (did something creatively different that led to an action and outcome)?

2. What recent examples of innovation come to mind with reference to your organization?

3. Are there any examples of innovation you are particularly proud of in your organization or sector of business?

4. How do you perceive innovation as ranked in importance within your organization's culture and approach?

5. How are creativity and innovation encouraged in your organization?

6. Does your organization expect innovation to be done by a specialized group of innovators or as part of what everyone does?

7. Can you think of some organizations you have come across that exhibit greater innovative behavior than yours?

Education

1. Do you have a mentor? Are you a mentor to others?

2. How do employees in your organization learn to follow the cultural norms and uphold the values of the organization?

3. Does your organization embark on educating other organizations (supplier, partner, customer, etc.) about its mission, ambitions, targets, values?

4. How often do you present at or attend trade shows, conferences or customer/partner events?

5. Are you aware of active online discussion forums relevant to your areas of specialism?

6. What established links does your organization have with education providers (e.g., schools and universities)?

7. Do you think schools and universities should be teaching differently based on what you have read here? If so, what and how should they be teaching differently?

Inspiration

1. Do you view yourself as inspirational? How could you become more inspirational to others?

2. What case studies or stories of organizations, teams or individuals doing great things can you share to inspire other colleagues?

3. Who and what naturally comes to mind when you think of inspiration within your organization?

4. If you could choose two people as your mentors out of all the people who have ever lived, who would they be, and why?

Techniques for Transformation

> Just do it!
>
> — Nike

EXECUTIVE SUMMARY

- A firm of the future is constantly transforming.
- The 5E cycle (see next page) is a dynamic process of activities within stages: explore, evaluate, envision, empower, execute.
- Explore the changing context and environment your organization operates in.
- Evaluate how your organization is performing against the changing context and goals.
- Envision what good could look like for your organization without being constrained, then apply the constraints of your business context to see what is a fit-for-purpose vision for your organization.
- Empower your people to make change happen and realize the goals.
- Execute your values and vision through right relations and right behavior.

We have explored the dynamic cycles of nature — how nothing is static, everything is constantly changing. With nature as our teacher, we have learned that a firm of the future is a business inspired by nature, and is aware of, aligned with and leverages the unpredictable dynamics of the systems within which it operates. We learned that a firm of the future is less about control and more about letting go; less about solving problems and more about working toward positive outcomes; less about static prescriptive protocols and more about descriptive dynamic and cyclic processes.

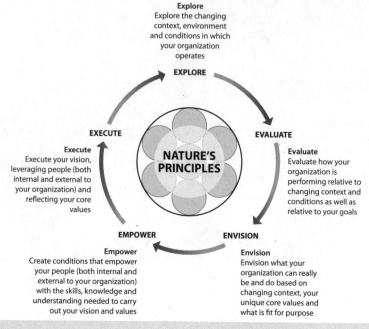

Figure 10. The 5E cycle.

In this module we look at how a business can develop its own dynamic and cyclic processes and techniques of transformation toward a firm of the future.

The 5E cycle

The 5E cycle, developed by Biomimicry for Creative Innovation (BCI), is a dynamic, continuous, cyclic process that businesses can follow to transform and continually inform themselves. The 5E cycle, and each step within it, is based on nature's business principles (explored in Module Three); it recognizes that nature has rules for sustainable operation and can provide guidance and inspiration that businesses can use to survive and thrive under volatile and unpredictable conditions within the finite limits of the Earth. Businesses can embed the 5E cycle into their management systems to achieve optimized performance, continual improvement toward positive outcomes and lasting resilience.

The 5E cycle starts with an exploration of and an inquiry into the complexity, dynamics and reality of the context and systems within which a business operates. It is about seeing the world holistically, as it really is, without the blinkers and filters of the conventional business worldview. Constantly exploring and understanding the changing nature of business reality helps a business more accurately evaluate how it is performing against all important factors now, and what changes may be needed to make it fit for purpose in future. Understanding and measuring business performance against "real" scales helps people start to envision what is really possible for their business — which is far greater than most imagine. This vision emerges from understanding and working with core values and risks, and finding new possibilities from change.

As in nature's cycles, the 5E cycle is a self-renewing process of continual sensing, adapting and evolving toward ever more positive outcomes. Also, as in nature's cycles, there is no beginning and no end. However, as your business embarks on its journey of transformation, it is helpful to begin by reflecting on where your business is now, where it ought to be and to envision the transformational journey. Use your inspiration, imagination and creativity to run through a few laps of the 5E cycle and see what as-yet-unimagined possibilities begin to emerge. The first tentative — or passionate — laps around the cycle will probably be clunky as you realize just how much of the firm-of-the-past thinking, habits, assumptions and limitations you may need to let go of. If possible, cycle through the steps with other like-minded individuals who are open to positive adaptation, awake to the interconnected nature of business reality, and willing to share and challenge, to move beyond the known and the doable into the unknowable and the positive; the potential, the as-yet-unimagined possible.

Explore

Every business operates within complex and constantly changing systems in which conditions of both human and natural systems are increasingly dynamic and unpredictable. Firms of the past work with limited light illuminating the path ahead, unaware of all the social, environmental and economic complexities and the full breadth and depth of changes that are occurring around them. This incomplete view of reality leaves businesses vulnerable to disruption and unable to sense and respond to unpredictable and emerging opportunities. In times of rapid change, businesses have a fundamental choice: explore and adapt to the full complexity and dynamics of their systems, or face the tough consequences.

A firm of the future continually explores, senses, responds, leverages and aligns itself with the human and natural systems within which it operates. Human systems reflect trends and disruptions (both positive and negative) in developing technologies, globalization, diversity, social responsibility and transparency. Changing trends and disruptions in natural systems include resource limitations, energy availability, climate change and environmental responsibility.

In the explore stage, you identify the components or aspects of the many systems within which your business operates and upon which your business depends, and then work to understand their dynamics. Explore how volatile, predictable, limiting or disruptable they might be. Explore the potential for sudden disruptions in supply, price spikes, radically new technologies, new legislation, political upheaval, natural disaster. Stretch the imagination and explore the potential for the unknown and unpredictable. If you find it hard to imagine such volatility in your conventional business environment, just review news headlines for the past twelve months.

Today, most businesses choose to ignore many crucial factors in their operating environment. For example, it is highly likely that the flow of petroleum supplies will be significantly and repeatedly disrupted within the business planning horizon (terrorist activities, natural disasters, climate change, political upheaval, diminishing easily available supplies, etc.). Virtually our entire economy is directly or indirectly reliant on a constant flow of petroleum, yet few businesses have explored the scope, scale or speed of such disruptions. Disruptions can be positive, too — just look how dramatically business has changed since the arrival of the Internet, mobile devices and social networking. We are all interconnected and interdependent, and changes within your business environment affect your organization and your business ecosystem. This then affects the whole system, in turn feeding back to affect your organization.

Systems thinking can be challenging for us to get our heads around; nature is composed of infinite complex interconnected ever-changing and unpredictable systems, and thus provides us with innumerable successful models for exploring, understanding and working with the complex and dynamic systems within which we operate. Business leaders and teams in the firm of the future engage in an enlightening process of exploration that looks at how performance can be inspired by nature rather than by a limited, reductionist approach to thinking. Exploring can start with insight into the full breadth of external factors that affect (or have the potential to affect) your business, your business environment and your business ecosystem within the months and years ahead, subject to your planning horizon.

In addition to exploring your external systems (the context in which your business and its respective ecosystem operates), you can also explore your business's internal systems. This means considering the unique dynamics of the resources and relationships you have within your organization. Firms of the past typically look at their human resources according to job titles and functions in the organization chart. Firms of the future consider the diversity of human nature represented within their stakeholder community. They realize that each job is filled by a unique human being with not only different skill sets and experience, but also different interests and passions, senses and sensibilities, values and value potential, with different antennae and modes of communication.

Your body is continuously exploring changes in your context and conditions. As you read this, for example, your body is continuously exploring your external environment, sensing changes in temperature, light, UV radiation, passage of diurnal and biological time, possible threats and innumerable other conditions. You are also continuously exploring your own internal conditions such as blood sugar and hunger, hydration and thirst, salinity, pH, temperature. This continuous exploration provides the information you need for the next step in the cycle: evaluate.

To get started, when exploring your internal resources, you may want to seek out the first crucial one percent of your people that can act as internal change agents and leaders in your transformation journey. These "one-percenters" are curious and creative, generous with ideas, naturally driven toward positive solutions, excited by the unpredictable and seek opportunities from disruptions. Once exposed to and trained in the concepts and tools highlighted in this book, your one-percenters will be empowered to sow and nourish seeds of change throughout your business and help guide your transformational journey.

Evaluate

Organisms in nature survive by continuously evaluating how well they fit relative to the changing conditions in which they live. Based on the feedback they get from a diversity of scales and sources, they respond and adapt accordingly, constantly moving toward positive outcomes.

Firms of the future continuously evaluate how well they are performing in, and aligning with, the contexts in which they operate; measuring what they value and valuing what they measure. Evaluating what's important in the long run as well as the short run allows a firm of the future to make the most of emerging opportunities, recover from disruptions and operate sustainably within all systems.

Firms of the past tend to evaluate their performance based on just two simple metrics: time and money. They value these two parameters and choose to ignore or be ignorant of all else, at best recognizing them as "externalities."

Evaluation helps leaders and teams assess how they are really doing comparatively (compared with the sector, industry, position, location), relatively (relative to the best that any business has to offer in any sector) and absolutely (against nature's principles) in a holistic way — qualitatively and quantitatively.

Effective evaluation starts with identifying the very real and specific challenges that already exist, as well as the opportunities emerging from your exploration of context. Effective evaluation of performance against reality leads into an assessment of how readily a business is prepared to address change, disruption and opportunity.

In the previous stage in the 5E cycle, you identified and explored the dynamics of the factors in your systems upon which your business depends and that have the potential to change. In the evaluate stage, you consider the range of possible impacts that such dynamics might have on your business, now and in the future, and how well-equipped your business is to respond with positive outcomes. What would happen to your business if gas supplies were cut off for a day? Or for five days? Ten days? If you think that your business is not gas-dependent, consider the fact that our food supply is dependent on gas, and you and your employees are entirely dependent on food — no gas, no food, no work.

One tool to use is what BCI calls a "resilience audit." The idea is to explore the breadth, depth and dynamics of systems in which your business participates, and consider how well your business can recover from potential disruptions in any of these systems. This is different from a risk assessment, where you calculate the probability of a disruptive event and then attempt to predict possible consequences, usually with the goal of protecting your business. Risk assessments work well with events that have happened repeatedly in the past and when the past is a good predictor of the future. Risk assessments are less useful for events that have not happened before, are highly unpredictable or are unimaginable through conventional thinking. In these cases, which are increasingly becoming the norm, the predict-and-protect approach has less value. A firm of the future chooses instead to evaluate and then build its resilience, its ability to recover from and leverage disturbance into opportunity.

> Your body uses the continual flow of information from exploration of its internal and external context to evaluate how well it is performing relative to current and potential future conditions, as well as relative to its ideal state of being or "vision." The comparison allows your body to determine what it needs and wants to do next.

Envision

Organizations inspired by nature create a vision based on a complete understanding of their dynamic context, respecting the scope, scale and speed of what needs to happen and by when, not limited in vision by their current position — a "pure vision" uncontaminated by conventional thinking. A "pure vision" strives to concurrently optimize abundance for the business and the systems within which it operates — the economic ecosystem, the community and natural ecosystems — while being uncontaminated by perceived limitations to what is possible. This can be a challenge for people in organizations shaped by conventional thinking absorbed within the prevailing business mindset.

Many people and businesses set goals based on an incomplete understanding of their context and limit themselves to what they think they can achieve based on partial understanding of the problems and challenges they believe they will face. For a business shaped by conventional thinking, the main goal — sometimes the sole goal — is to maximize short-term profit. This approach will not — and cannot — lead to an innovative sustainable resilient business. In a firm of the future, envisioning reflects a holistic understanding of reality, the unique values of the business, how well the business is currently performing, what is fit for purpose, and what is truly possible.

As in nature, a pure vision doesn't emerge from analysing and solving perceived problems and challenges. It is based instead on knowing what "good" looks like and continually moving toward positive outcomes. A pure vision unleashes employees' full creative potential and passion, giving them the energy and confidence to seek dynamic, engaging and innovative solutions.

Envisioning puts aside all current constraints and focuses on how a business and its ecosystem can be inspired by nature and redesigned in the most optimal way, fit for purpose and ready to flourish within the ever-changing environment. With pure vision in mind, a business can then overlay the realities identified in the explore and evaluate stages to understand potential for "quick wins," "systemic change" and "radical transformation" shaped by the pure vision based on your unique reality.

How does a business create a pure vision? BCI suggests that you start by first ranking your business on a scale of 1 to 10 in terms of business performance, sustainability, employee well-being and empowerment, community and stakeholder engagement, resource efficiency —

whatever factors your business thinks are important (as long as they are holistic and complete in nature; incompleteness at this stage of the journey is not good). Let's call this scale P1 to P10, with P indicating past or present thinking. On this scale, P1 is the lowest level that is compliant or otherwise passable and P10 is what is considered best in class based on conventional thinking. For example, P1 might be releasing the maximum level of toxic waste into the air, water or soil that a business might be able to get away with legally. P10 might be zero-emissions, zero-waste or zero carbon.

A firm of the future recognizes that the real scale extends far beyond P10 to a "real 10," or R10, with "real" referring to what is really needed in terms of both performance and consciousness to be a business inspired by nature, aligned with nature, synergistic with nature and fit for purpose for the world we now live in if we are to survive and thrive. For example, an R10 vision far surpasses "zero" as a goal and imagines a business as actively contributing to virtuous cycles within every system in which it operates. It envisions the world as it should be and as it can be, and then envisions its activities in that world. Ian Cheshire, Chief Executive of B&Q, has noted that:

> Infinite high-resource-intensity growth is simply not possible, and we are already living off our future capital. It may be gradual but most businesses will have to adjust to a very different reality. That reality will still be a version of capitalism, and needs to be a positive vision rather than a doom-laden return to the Stone Age, but it needs to rethink the point of the system. Instead of the goal of maximum linear growth in GDP, we should be thinking of maximum well-being for minimal planetary input.[1]

At any given timescale, your body has an ideal state or "vision." Your body's vision and goals for itself as a small child are quite different from its vision for itself now. The ideal state for you when you are outside and active in the wintertime is quite different from the ideal state for you when you are sitting inside a warm room.

Empower

For businesses shaped by conventional thinking, HR management can be seen as "filling the org chart," squeezing the most out of human resources for lowest cost using the latest management techniques, retaining "high performers" through status and pay structures. External to the organization, a firm of the past works the supply chain, making deals to maximize revenue, minimize cost and expand market share. All relationships — including those with their own customers, shareholders and employees — are considered fundamentally competitive, at best win–win. People are controlled and managed by leaders who often think of themselves as lecturers, loners and heroes.

Businesses inspired by nature empower people by exploring, fostering and leveraging individual and collective diversity, creativity, feedback loops and free energy of their human resources. A business inspired by nature makes the most of the unique characteristics and capacities of each person. Organizational structures inspired by nature are fluid and dynamic, allowing self-assembly that fits form to function. Relationships with employees, customers, shareholders, stakeholders and the extended business ecosystem are based on synergies designed for creating abundance and resilience (win–win–win as a minimum). Leaders are hosts, facilitators, catalysts and listeners.

The empowering stage of the 5E cycle requires business leaders (and the one-percenters discussed earlier) to focus on creating conditions that enable people to transform the vision into reality. Business leaders use inspiration from nature to transform their own leadership style in order to unleash, fully empower and optimize their people (and the business's ecosystem community) to make the change real. They live, share and spread the inspiration of transformation to continually reenergize the courage needed to make change happen.

Empowering employees requires exploring new ways of working together collaboratively and co-creatively toward your vision. The Applied Improvisation Network has developed a set of very useful, practical and easy-to-use tools and techniques that can greatly facilitate this new way of working together.[2] For example, when a group is empowered to come up with new ideas or solutions, participants take a "Yes, and…" approach, meaning they begin each comment or response by first acknowledging what they like about the new idea ("Yes, what I like about that is…") and then add what they think would help move that idea toward the positive outcome or vision ("and…"). A "Yes, and" discussion is creative, fun, empowering and generates innovative thinking and solutions. This is in stark contrast to the conventional "No, because" or "Yes, but" approaches, which tend to be offensive/defensive, demoralizing and often result in highlighting limitations and what "can't" be done rather than possible ways forward.

Creative thinking techniques covered in Module Five also help create the conditions for empowering change to happen. This is just as much about listening and sowing the seeds of confidence in others as it is about proactively stimulating creativity. In hand with this is providing a safe environment for yourself and others to fail, and so learn and grow. Stillness, presence, appreciation and empathy are all vital ingredients here. In the words of Nancy Kline, "the quality of your attention determines the quality of other people's thinking." [3] Hence, empowering leadership styles may include techniques such as meditation, effective listening and coaching skills.

Empowerment is a key driver of the virtuous cycles envisioned in the previous stage. Once empowered, your employees and your expanding network of stakeholders begin to recognize how they can optimally contribute to your business, to your R10 and to the systems within which your business operates.

After your body updates its vision, it empowers itself (if it is not already empowered) to carry out the vision. If it senses a drop in blood sugar, your body empowers you to take action with a sense of hunger and appetite. If you sense imminent danger, it releases adrenaline to enable fight or flight. If you sense "good vibes" with another, your body's emotions help create conditions conducive to positive interaction.

Execute

Businesses execute their vision through their people, processes, products and places, as well as through the relations with the human and natural systems within which they operate. The actions of businesses shaped by conventional thinking are typically short-term, profit-focused and risk-based, which limits innovation and is therefore unsustainable in the long term.

The people, processes, products and places of businesses inspired by nature are grounded in nature's principles, and are thus both innovative and sustainable. A business inspired by nature recognizes the many ways it interacts with human and natural systems, and takes action to align with, support and leverage both.

The actions of businesses inspired by nature are forward-looking, continually moving toward individual and collective positive outcomes creating abundance for themselves and for their systems.

Execution is the implementation and realization of dynamic, transformative change at the people, process, product and place levels, using nature for inspiration. The positive results of these actions drive the transformation forward, and the self-renewing, self-energizing positive virtuous 5E cycle continues. As you enter the explore and evaluate steps of the next cycle, you can take stock, seeing how far you have come on your transformational journey, learning lessons while recognizing and celebrating short-term successes along the way to much greater goals.

Questions

1. Is your organization already embarking upon a transformation of some form?

2. Is it clear what the transformational journey of your organization is about, what the values and vision are?

3. How do you feel about the level of transformational change in your organization? Is it scary? Is it encouraging? Is it chaotic? Is it timely? Does it feel right?

4. What do you see as your role within the organization's transformation?

5. Try doing a simple resilience audit for your organization by listing the external factors that could affect your organization's performance over the next twelve months. What approaches are in place to help ensure these changing environmental factors become opportunities?

6. What does the R10 "pure vision" look like for your organization?

7. Can you think of any organizations similar to your organization that are embarking upon significant transformation? How successful are their transformations so far?

8. Do you know of people within your organization and also partner organizations who could help drive transformation forward in the next twelve months?

9. How would you go about selecting and engaging your organization's one percent?

Inspiration for Transformation

> If you want to go quickly, go alone.
> If you want to go far, go together.
>
> — Ancient African proverb

EXECUTIVE SUMMARY

:• Adnams, Ecover, Tata and Virgin are all showing "resilience" in difficult market conditions.

:• Each company seeks to improve upon nature's business principles in different ways, each facing different business challenges ahead of them.

:• Adnams and Ecover are good examples of medium-sized businesses striving toward business as a force for good.

:• Tata and Virgin are good examples of multinational conglomerates with strong ethics, yet continual challenges to ensure values are not jeopardized by short-term business desires.

As we have noted, the firm of the future is not a prescriptive model, but rather a compass of principles to help navigate an optimal transformational journey, just as the 5E cycle is not a prescriptive cookbook to control a staged transformation but a guiding approach to actively enacting dynamic change. There is no cookbook or prescriptive model for future transformation, only guidance, principles, practices and good business sense. We are all on our own individual and collective journeys toward the future — one which, through our awareness and conviction, can be a positive, life-giving transformation or an unsustainable, life-damaging one. To that end, there are a number of organizations (some mentioned already), of various sectors and sizes, that are on a journey of transformation toward their own version of a firm of the future — some aspects

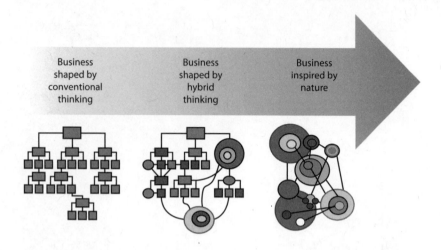

Figure 11. The journey of transformation.

of each transformation may be incremental and others more radical, subject to the courage, conviction and circumstances of those affecting change within these organizations.

Four case studies have been selected, not because they represent firms of the future but because each brings different insights, and so provides inspiration and learning for our own organizational transformations. None of these organizations would profess to be perfect in any way and all recognize they are on their own unique transformational paths. The organizations are:

- Adnams — a small brewery based in the UK.
- Ecover — a medium-sized consumer goods manufacturer based in Belgium.
- Tata — a conglomerate of a number of different organizations connected through the Tata Corporation, based in India.
- Virgin — a conglomerate of a number of different organizations connected through the Virgin Group, based in the UK.

Adnams

Adnams was founded in 1872 by George and Ernest Adnams in Southwold, Suffolk. The company produces cask ale, pasteurized bottled beer and spirits, including gin, vodka and whisky. Adnams extends to a chain of hotels, pubs and Cellar and Kitchen shops.

Adnams has a long history of placing values at the heart of its business. Holistic social, environmental and economic values build a strong organizational culture. Such values have been the driving force behind the company's approach to people, process, product and place, with a number of notable organizational changes in recent years.

For example, the Adnams distribution center (DC) solves sustainability issues using practices taken from nature, which in turn generates greater efficiency within the company. Adnams has built its DC from "hemcrete," made from lime and local hemp. These natural materials lock in high levels of carbon dioxide in the blocks to help regulate the temperature in the building, thus removing the need for refrigeration or heating to maintain a constant temperature of 13°C. This has saved around 600 tons of CO_2 compared with more energy-intensive building materials such as concrete. A green roof on the DC reduces the visual impact of the building and helps regulate its internal temperature. Two solar panels provide 80 percent of the distribution center's hot water. Steam from the brewing process ("brewstream"), is captured to heat the following brew, which cuts gas usage by 30 percent.

Rainwater is collected and used to flush toilets and to wash the company vehicles. The range of eco-features at Adnams differentiates it from traditional brewing companies. Also, Adnams has developed biogas production using anaerobic digestion (AD), which uses waste from the brewery, pubs, restaurants and retailers locally to make biomethane. The gas is used to power Adnams' distribution center and brew-house, and some has also been fed back to the National Grid. Ultimately it will be used to power the commercial vehicle fleet. The plant will use around 12,500 tons of organic waste per year to produce up to 4.8 million kilowatt-hours; this is enough to heat around 235 homes for a year. The scheme diverts food waste from entering landfill sites and prevents the release of methane, a highly polluting greenhouse gas, into the atmosphere (equivalent to 50,000 tons of CO_2). The AD plant is powered by 0.5 kW of solar panels, with residue energy used to operate the DC or feed into the grid.

Let's look at the Adnams business through the lenses of nature's business principles.

Resilient

Adnams was able to leverage the shock of the 2008–9 economic crisis as an opportunity. It sensed and responded, rather than dwelled, and utilized the opportunity to reassess the way in which business works during a cultural and attitudinal shift. Investing in business in difficult times, along with making bold changes toward more diversity in its business model, allowed it to move into adjacent markets, such as spirits. Adnams also evolved from dealing 25 percent of volume with two big customers toward an ecosystem of smaller customers, providing significant increased resilience in difficult market conditions. Staff empowerment and stakeholder-engagement initiatives encourage people to make local decisions more effectively, leading to more distributed decision-making. In this period, while the core market declined due to the economic climate and the switch from on- to off-trade, a more diverse product and client portfolio led to short-term improvements, while embedding strategic resilience into the business. During this time of change, Adnams has outperformed the market in terms of beer volumes sold.

Optimizing

Just prior to the economic crisis, Adnams reorganized into smaller, more siloed business functions (for example, sales, marketing, human resources). At a time when rapid change and collaboration was needed to deal with the external threat of the global crisis, it quickly sensed the reduction in synergies brought about through the separation of business functions and the reduced collaboration between parts of the business. Sensing and responding to this quickly, it returned to a more integrated functional approach, where economies of scope were realized more readily through interdependent connection between stakeholders and the fostering of local empowerment. Adnams, through experience and feedback from its stakeholder community, has sought to find the right balance of economies of scale and scope fit for purpose for its business model and culture — optimizing rather than maximizing. Interestingly, other breweries have chosen the more prevailing paradigm of economies of scale over scope, which, while gaining short-term cost savings in places, can lead to a diminution of the strategic resilience that is so fundamental in these volatile times.

Adaptive

The development of eco-efficiency infrastructure and processes, design inspired by nature and symbiotic research links with the University of East Anglia makes Adnams more able to adapt to the cost variabilities of raw materials and energy, while encouraging a more eco-aware business environment for all stakeholders. Adnams has developed strong relationships with local farms, which support the farmers and the brewers during environmental challenges, such as drought (Adnams is located in one of the driest parts of the UK).

Also, changes in customer base and product portfolio have ensured adaptation to market conditions. The investments Adnams has made in transforming its operational and business practices are now paying off through a more adaptive and responsive overall business.

System-based

Adnams has a network of around 70 pubs, 1,200 stockists and outlets, and a growing customer community — all of these form a part of the vibrant ecosystem. Social media plays a growing part of the stakeholder community feel, with a large following on Twitter and Facebook. This is used as a feedback mechanism, rather than a marketing tool, as it creates an interactive dialogue and develops trust between Adnams and its stakeholders.

In nature, waste of one becomes food for another. Adnams is trying to follow this logic in its approach to its stakeholder ecosystem, its people, processes, products and infrastructure. This is a continuing process, as the business still produces waste that is not yet fully utilized; yet there is a focus on zero-waste. Nature-inspired systems-thinking initiatives (such as the use of solar, anaerobic digestion turning waste into renewable gas going back to the grid and the reuse of wastewater for farm fertilizers) form part of this zero-waste approach. Adnams is on the journey toward creating an industrial ecology with its customers, suppliers and other stakeholders.

Values-led

Adnams has consistently upheld its values to be a socially and environmentally aware business. Ventures include taking part in the Marine Conservation Society's "adopt a beach" scheme, replacing all the bulbs in the Adnams hotels with low-energy alternatives, using biodegradable plastic bags in its stores, switching to a waste supplier with a larger recycling threshold and working toward the ISO 14001 environmental standard. Adnams' values have been taken to its extended network of pubs, which have hugely influenced the human aspect and business performance of this network.

Adnams is involved in numerous projects concerned with nature conservation and enhancing quality of life within its local community. The company's Chairman, Jonathan Adnams, received an OBE from the Queen in 2009 due to the organization's commitment to society and the environment. It is this strong values-led culture that ensures all Adnams' staff are proud and committed to the long-term development of the company. This connection with strong values also extends to the wider stakeholder community of suppliers, partners, customers and investors alike.

Life-supporting

Through a combination of long- and short-term goals, Adnams hopes to move toward no carbon emissions and sending nothing to landfill. Adnams recognizes that currently there are too many life-damaging aspects in business, and it wants to identify and eliminate these while creating conditions conducive to life in all aspects of its business. Adnams recognizes the symbiotic nature of business working with local community projects and takes an active part in a number of non-profit initiatives (for example, Business in the Community[1]).

As a result of all these nature-inspired and values-led initiatives, Adnams is out-performing its market, showing volume growth of 4 percent year on year, while the market declines by 4 percent year on year. Good business sense prevails.

Ecover

Ecover manufactures and internationally trades ecological cleaning products for both domestic and professional use. It is currently the world's leading manufacturer of ecological cleaning products, providing innovative plant-based products with reusable, recyclable and renewable packaging. In 1980, it started as a small company producing phosphate-free products sold exclusively to health-food stores. It now produces a wide range of ecological products covering cleaning, personal care and washing. These products are distributed globally, with the most important markets being Europe (United Kingdom, Benelux, Germany) and the United States.

In 1992, Ecover built the world's first "ecological factory." With a surface area of around 8,000 m², it houses sophisticated equipment and handles large volumes for a production capacity of 15,000 tons per year. The factory has many sustainable elements, a green roof and green electricity. The 6,000 m² green roof is formed of thick *Sedum* (or "thunder beard" as it is known), which gives effective insulation all year round. The walls are constructed using a special type of brick which is made from a mixture of clay, wood pulp and pit coal dust. The brick-firing process requires less energy, and these bricks are light and porous after firing, with good thermal insulating properties. They are formed of recycled materials, such as wall blocks made from colliery waste. In 2007, a second factory was constructed in the north of France, which used similar but more modern techniques.

Ecover recently developed an alternative packaging solution that is entirely renewable, reusable and recyclable. "Plant-astic" is made from sugarcane that is harvested to produce sugar, which is then fermented and distilled to produce ethanol. The ethanol is then dehydrated to create ethylene, which is polymerized into the final Plant-astic product. The sugarcane is sourced from sustainable plantations, and the efficient production process means that only fifteen hectares of land need harvesting to make a year's worth of Ecover packaging. Although some types of biodegradable plastic are already available, they are not always suitable for long-term storage of Ecover's products. An active research program into alternative packaging materials is therefore indispensable.

Resilient

Ecover has developed a niche in a very competitive and highly volatile global consumer goods market by providing environmentally responsible products, which differentiates it from competitors. It sells through a diverse range of specialized and mass distribution channels (health stores, e-commerce, social media, mass retail, etc.). By diversifying its distribution between specialized and mass channels, it has become less exposed to market volatility. Greater product diversity, continual innovation and improvements in the quality of environmentally responsible products through a values-led approach ensure customer retention and growth in difficult market conditions. This continual innovation and diversification (personal and non-personal care product ranges), focused on the value to the customer in terms of quality and environmental responsibility, enables Ecover to remain a leader in an increasingly competitive niche.

Optimizing

Continual improvement and optimization are embedded in the culture, as any new product brought to market must have an additional value for their ISO 14001 environmental-management standard, or an improvement on an earlier model or market standard, ensuring continual improvement against the organizational goal of improving the environmental responsibility of all products.

Ecover has developed the Diamond model as a tool to evaluate the impact of the total life cycle of its products. The Ecover Diamond is divided into thirteen axes of quantifiable characteristics within three main processes: sourcing; use and performance; and absorption and waste. By measuring all aspects of the product life cycle, the optimization of the product is directed toward a holistic, environmentally responsible approach, where all aspects of the life cycle are integrated into the business decision-making and none is "externalized" as not being the responsibility of Ecover. Interestingly, Ecover does not limit this holistic approach to the product life cycle but also applies it to all aspects of its business (human resources, accounting, etc.) to help ensure that the whole organization (and its ecosystem, where possible) evolves toward a more sustainable future.

Adaptive

Ecover has multiple distribution channels, operating in mass markets and niche markets, some new markets and some stable. Its products are altered according to large cultural, environmental and usage differences between markets (e.g., hard or soft water variables, subject to geographic market, or differences in approaches to washing depending on the prevalent culture in that market). This market diversity is embraced by Ecover as an opportunity to provide specific value, with products being market-attuned where possible. Locally attuned market knowledge, intelligence and feedback allow Ecover to continually adapt to specific market characteristics and changing needs. This adaptability is natural for any successful fast-moving-consumer-goods company, and on top of this, Ecover ensures a good level of adaptivity through effective responsiveness to supplier and customer feedback with open, connected stakeholder relations, as we see in the following section.

System-based

In approaching environmental awareness and improvement policies, all parts of the organization are engaged. The environmental management system is applied across all departments and to partners and other stakeholders that engage with Ecover, where possible. Views of all partners and aspects of the organization are gathered to gain a holistic view, with many of the suppliers actively engaged in collaborative working with Ecover. Research institutes, universities and R&D from other partners all engage synergistically to help drive systemic transformation in the business ecosystem wherever possible.

For example, in developing biodegradable bottles made from sustainably sourced sugarcane, collaboration is needed from parties involved in growing and harvesting through to research and development of package design. A new packaging process Ecover implemented with one supplier allowed distribution boxes to be folded and reused rather than destroyed and recycled. This system was later installed by the supplier across other organizations they supplied, allowing the benefits to extend beyond Ecover's ecosystem, while enhancing the resilience of its own ecosystem by helping its supplier provide additional systemic value.

Creating an open environment among stakeholders, where sharing and collaboration is encouraged, is fundamental to ensuring Ecover stays at the forefront of its market and continues to provide the best value it can for its customers. As Ecover is a relatively small player in a highly competitive consumer goods market, it needs the collaborative assistance of its partners to drive innovation in the most cost-effective way. This collaboration extends to its customers, and through social media, it has organized customer judging panels for new products and their ingredients and fragrances. Also, customers can test new products and ingredients, providing direct feedback, while also sharing this feedback with other customers. This is co-creation in the making and is very exciting for Ecover. In the future, open-source development and transparent research will be crucial for Ecover.

Values-led

Ecover's central aim is to bring efficient and sustainable products to the market for people today and for future generations. It seeks to contribute to the process of creating economical, ecological and social change within society to build a sustainable future for everyone. It aims to maximize the use of renewable ingredients, continually striving for 100 percent wherever possible.

It has strong company values of commitment, respect and integrity, which are integrated into all teams across the organization, and where possible it actively educates and integrates values with partner and supplier organizations too. Renewability, respect for animals and life, and finding alternatives to testing on animals are important issues that are frequently discussed with suppliers to find solutions. Sometimes it is very difficult to educate suppliers in such areas due to the ingrained nature of the prevalent mindset across business, meaning many organizations find it difficult to accept that "respect for life" is an important issue. Ecover screens suppliers regularly through values-based criteria aligned to Ecover's values, and if not satisfied with the supplier's performance on these values, it will select an alternative supplier, even if that means additional financial expense to the business.

Likewise, all staff are given the opportunity to develop their individual knowledge, skills and training, and have a strong understanding and acceptance of the values of the organization — in many instances it is the main motivator for working for the organization.

Life-supporting

From its ecological factory, with its green roof, its "respect for life" approach in its products and supply chain, through to its sourcing of materials in a sustainable way, Ecover aligns with nature wherever possible. Using customers in product design and ingredient selection helps with customer awareness and encourages constant innovation in realizing Ecover's mission — to provide products that are conducive to life. Continually exceeding market standards helps inspire others in the market by acting as a case study of what can be achieved, and also by helping drive systemic change toward more sustainable business practices.

Tata

There are twenty-eight publicly listed Tata enterprises. The major Tata companies are Tata Steel, Tata Motors, Tata Consultancy Services (TCS), Tata Power, Tata Chemicals, Tata Global Beverages, Indian Hotels and Tata Communications. Every Tata company or enterprise operates independently. Each of these companies has its own board of directors and shareholders, to whom it is answerable. Connecting the Tata enterprises are the Group Executive Office (GEO) and the Group Corporate Centre (GCC), which define and direct the business endeavours of the Tata Group.

Sixty-five percent ownership of Tata Sons Ltd, the main holding company for the group, is held by charitable trusts set up by previous generations of the Tata family who have stewarded the group since its creation in 1868. The Tata Council for Community Initiatives (TCCI) has been created around a unique concept based on participatory networking to facilitate the Tata Group's diversity of work in the areas of community outreach, social programs, biodiversity, environment management and employee voluntarism. It also encourages innovations that take place in these areas to influence business strategy and practices. The TCCI institutionalizes good business sense across the Tata Group and has enabled and facilitated organizations to migrate from good philanthropic practices to an understanding of sustainability as good business sense, highlighting its critical importance for the long-term progress of each organization and the Group as a whole.

> The TCCI encourages a bottom-up form of engagement and assists companies to help evolve their own direction and opportunities to foster this work more systematically. There is no formal mandate of any kind—hoping it would also largely be driven by the employees who responsibly think, initiate and do this work. So, senior directors, CEOs, executives, facilitators, volunteers and employees actually form the TCCI by their sheer conviction, love, dedication and active involvement for this work. It is based on initiative and voluntarism of associates.
> — ANANT G. NADKARNI, TATA SERVICES[2]

> I think that the message we would like to leave with our CEOs is that there is an integrated approach—that we want them to be profit-oriented, we want them to be cost-effective, we want them to be quality-conscious, and we want them to be good corporate citizens.
> — RATAN TATA, CHAIRMAN, TATA SERVICES[3]

Resilient

The Tata Group is a diverse family of companies, all independent in their own right, yet connected through values and governance, and hence "interdependent." This decentralized, diverse family of companies has weathered volatile market conditions, growing by seeking out opportunities in this volatility. Resilience is core to the Tata Group. For example, Tata Chemicals anticipated pressure on profits after the Beijing Olympics and put in place a program called "Action plan for Downturn Alleviation and Profiting in Turbulence" (Adapt). Circumstances changed, and the plan was modified accordingly. Tata Chemical's success in weathering the current recession has been attributed in large part to this resilience program.

Optimizing

While Tata embraces the benefits of economies of scale, it also explores the opportunities of economies of scope to balance scale where appropriate. Working with local partners and diverse stakeholder communities is how Tata likes to operate.

An example of optimization within the business is where Tata pioneered a new model for supply chain optimization, together with partner Wallenius Wilhelmsen Logistics (WWL), making a critical addition to the three traditional optimization factors of lead time, cost and quality by including carbon emissions. New calculation and optimization tools were developed, proving that significant carbon emissions and cost savings can be achieved through optimization.

At the heart of Tata's approach to business optimization is culture that instils leadership, local attunement and empowerment into its people.

> Each person is unique. Each group, community and situation is unique. So are businesses and their cultures. What is underpinning is that leadership is about everybody making the true choices: business as usual or should we do it differently? Should we be proactive or should we wait till we are forced by circumstances? Should we lead by our own capacity to act (first be the change), or just manipulate our way? Are we interested in mere compliance or genuinely committed to the well-being of our employees and people in the community?
>
> — ANANT G. NADKARNI[4]

Tata has set up a corporate sustainability (CS) leadership profile and process to co-create sustainable value across the group and challenge personal, intellectual and institutional frontiers for each and all to optimize toward improved sustainable value creation, collaboration and leadership. CS leadership is mainly about:

+ Leading by example, experimenting with oneself, trying new things and testing ideas.
+ The ability to demonstrate conviction and commitment, with initiative as the driver.
+ Recognizing the power of consensus. Whether it is in board meetings, strategy conclaves, supplier/dealer seminars, employee councils or stakeholder consultations, there is sound faith in leveraging the "collective wisdom."
+ Valuing the importance of using personality and self-expression — emotional, creative, aesthetic, intuitive, social and spiritual persona — over and above normal cognitive intelligence.

These perspectives help each Tata organization to look at any proposal from different angles, optimizing to the dynamic environment. This approach helps overcome fear of change and helps instil courage for transformation (personal and organizational).

Adaptive

Through its approach to innovation, Tata constantly seeks adaptation to the volatile business environments it operates in. Ranked 17th in *Bloomberg Businessweek*'s "World's Most Innovative Companies 2010," Tata "takes innovation so seriously that it has developed an 'innometer.' The conglomerate measures creative goals and accomplishments vs domestic or global benchmarks while instilling a 'sense of urgency' among employees."[5]

Another example of adaptation is the Tinplate Company of India (TCIL), another part of the Tata Group, which used flexible production runs and short- to medium-term pricing strategies to weather the 2008–9 crisis.

Tata Group, through TCCI and Tata Quality Management Services (TQMS), ensures there is effective, responsive stakeholder engagement and feedback at all levels within each organization. Self-evaluation, process-maturation modelling and knowledge management within each company and across the group all help ensure stakeholders feed into, learn, adapt and respond to changing business conditions. This process of stakeholder engagement identifies concerns, expectations and needs, helping the systematic capture of feedback from the people and wider community of stakeholders. This builds effective organizational and group learning, improving adaptability through systemic sensing and responding.

Tata's business activities are not always viewed as providing holistic value. It has on occasions had to adapt to feedback from local communities and pressure groups. For example, Tata Motors ceased "nano car" production as a result of social unrest. Here, the West Bengal government gave 997 acres of some of the most fertile land of Singur to Tata Motors for factory development. The development would have ultimately resulted in the eviction of an estimated 15,000 farmers and the loss of the agricultural land. Tata Motors said they had come to West Bengal hoping to add value and prosperity and to create job opportunities in the communities in the state. Yet they ended up abandoning plans for the factory due to protests and social unrest.

It is also worth mentioning that a number of products within Tata Group are not adapting as fast as they could due to market trends; for example, cars still running solely on gas rather than adapting to more sustainable car design and development. Tata Motors has been making conscious efforts in the implementation of several environmentally sensitive technologies in the manufacturing processes. The company uses some of the world's most advanced equipment to check and control emissions. Yet being involved with a diverse selection of industries means Tata needs to ensure it is constantly adapting and innovating along with or ahead of some of the best in those markets (Toyota and BMW, for instance, in the car industry).

Systems-based

At the root of Tata's approach to business is how it operates within a community of mutually beneficial relations. From its inception, Tata has remained very aware of its business ecosystem and the wider stakeholder communities within which it operates. The Tata Business Excellence Model (TBEM) is a framework used across the group for integrating process standards and embedding values across all business operations.

Across the group, synergies have been gained (TCS and Tata Communications, for example) where respective parts of the group gain synergies with other parts of the group. The symbiotic nature of partnerships across the diverse business ecosystem is fundamental to the resilience of each organization's survival within the group. Tata endeavors to take a holistic approach in developing its partnership ecosystem, ensuring there are partnerships for better environmental management, environmental education initiatives, disaster-management strategies, understanding biodiversity linkages to livelihoods and the overall economy, ensuring social, environmental and economic partnership values are included in its ecosystem. Partnerships with research institutes, business schools and universities are well established as a vital way to collaborate and build understanding on economic, social and environmental trends.

For example, recently there has been a flourishing partnership between Tata and the Saïd Business School in Oxford, bringing opportunities in research and teaching while providing a bridge across the worlds of business and academia on issues such as sustainability, supply chain and macroeconomic trends. In short, Tata views partnerships and stakeholder relations as key to developing new ways of working across every aspect of business.

In the words of Professor Mervyn E. King (GRI): "The Tata Group has for years been carrying on business as unusual, in the sense that they have had regard to the impacts which their businesses have had on the communities in which they operate and the environment."[6]

Values-led

The Tata Group positions itself as a values-driven institution with sustainability at its core. Tata has a longstanding commitment to its business ecosystem of stakeholders, with trust based on values at the root of these successful mutually enhancing stakeholder relations. The values of trust, integrity and the greater good of humankind run across the entire group.

Tata's values are:

+ **Integrity:** We must conduct our business fairly, with honesty and transparency. Everything we do must stand the test of public scrutiny.

+ **Understanding:** We must be caring, show respect, compassion and humanity for our colleagues and customers around the world, and always work for the benefit of the communities we serve.

+ **Excellence:** We must constantly strive to achieve the highest possible standards in our day-to-day work and in the quality of the goods and services we provide.

+ **Unity:** We must work cohesively with our colleagues across the group and with our customers and partners around the world, building strong relationships based on tolerance, understanding and mutual cooperation.

+ **Responsibility:** We must continue to be responsible, sensitive to the countries, communities and environments in which we work, always ensuring that what comes from the people goes back to the people many times over.[7]

Unlike many corporate values charters, the values at Tata are inherent in business behavior. Tata is clear to point out that it is not business first and values second; it is values that direct and shape business behavior. While Tata Group is a good example of a values-led group of organizations, the group would be the first to admit that this approach is a journey of continuous learning and improvement, with plenty of opportunities to do things better in the continual strive toward excellence.

> Our purpose within the Tata Group is to improve the quality of life of the community we serve. And with an increased awareness of our surroundings, both physical and spiritual, we can contribute a great deal by making life a fulfilling, rewarding journey.
> — T. R. Doongaji[8]

It is equally important to point out that some of Tata's business activities in India and further afield test the values of its own values-driven institution. As mentioned earlier, for example, the incident of Tata Motors acquiring land in Singur for car production, which would ultimately have led to the eviction of farmers from productive agricultural land, caused social unrest and questions of economic, environmental and social motives to be raised. Tata Group, as a worldwide conglomerate, needs to be ever vigilant that its business desires for growth and market expansion do not lead to the undermining of social and environmental ethics embedded in its values. Hence, Tata is constantly challenged to ensure that, not just in theory but also in practice, it is never a case of business first and values second.

Life-supporting

Tata companies believe in returning wealth to the society they serve. Two-thirds of the equity of Tata Sons, the Tata promoter company, is held by philanthropic trusts that have created national institutions for science and technology, medical research, social studies and the performing arts. The trusts also provide aid and assistance to nongovernment organizations working in the areas of education, healthcare and livelihoods. Tata companies also extend social welfare activities to communities around their industrial units. The combined development-related expenditure of the trusts and the companies amounts to around 4 percent of the net profits of all the Tata companies taken together.

The group's contribution to conservation falls into two categories: first, the efforts of different Tata companies, big and small, to preserve and enrich the environment in and around their areas of operation; and, second, the TCCI Group initiative and the philanthropic thrust of the Tata trusts, which support a diverse cluster of nongovernmental organizations working in areas such as the management of natural resources, community development and livelihoods. This dual canopy accommodates and nurtures a variety of initiatives in a range that extends from watershed programs and land regeneration to forestry projects and the protection of endangered species.

> I have been lucky to work with organizations that truly believe in holistic and inclusive growth, ranging from voluntary work to the private sector. One appreciates how intrinsically society and

enterprise are linked only when one gets into the thick of both. Here with the Tatas I am working closely with various other stakeholders to bridge the distances to create a mutually beneficial future. Like the Tatas, I believe that marrying prosperity, wellness and business growth with paucity, lack of opportunity and access to development is the only way forward for a happy, healthy and mutually beneficial future.

— Foram Nagori[9]

An example of life-supporting activities is Tata Motors using wastewater and rainwater harvesting from its operations to transform 800 acres of arid land into a biodiverse wildlife habitat, through years of tree planting, habitat restoration and investment. Tata Motors was awarded the Bombay Natural History Society (BNHS) Green Governance Award. This "legacy of love" for biodiversity and ecosystems, inspired by Tata Motors, has germinated other Tata initiatives across India, and now in other parts of the globe where Tata operates.

Another example of life-supporting activities is Tata Power planting millions of saplings. This forestation initiative has not only helped in increasing the water-retention capability and rejuvenation of natural springs but has also helped in conserving the flora and fauna. According to Malcolm Lane, Director of Corporate Affairs with TCS and Regional Coordinator with Europe Regional Group: "Jamsetji Tata, a man of faith, used good thoughts, good words and good deeds and his business skill to build a firm foundation for subsequent generations and why should we aim to do anything less?"[10]

Just as a balanced reflective view is needed when looking at values with regard to Tata's immense business operations, so too is balanced reflection needed when looking at life-supporting activities. While Tata clearly embraces a number of life-supporting activities, it is fair to say that a number of its core business operations are far from life-supporting in that they negatively impact life through pollution and toxic by-products. Unfortunately, heavy industries (like car and steel making, which Tata operates in) are still very much rooted in the "take–make–waste" approach to manufacturing, causing significant damage to nature, and so to the wider fabric of life.

Virgin

Virgin has created more than 400 branded companies worldwide, employing approximately 60,000 people in 30 countries. The company operates in many diverse business sectors, most notably travel, media, health, leisure and finance, having operations in Europe, North America, Asia, Australia and Africa.

Virgin operates as a structure of loosely linked autonomous units run by self-managed teams that share a brand name and values. Interestingly (and unlike most other large businesses) Virgin does not have an organizational chart on its website. Partly, the group is so diverse that it would be difficult to depict this graphically, but it is also not in Virgin's culture to think in "org chart" terms. The model is decentralized, with units making their own business decisions as appropriate for their market conditions; they have the benefit of autonomy coupled with the benefit—where and when it is needed—of scale and scope.

There is no central HQ, nor are financials consolidated for a group view. The only central function is Virgin Management Ltd, which provides advisory services to all companies within the group and also has specialist sector and regional teams.

Virgin's founder, Richard Branson, is viewed with suspicion by some in the City as a wildcard because he shuns the established business norm and creates new structures that do not always conform to traditional analyst models. At the same time, his motivational leadership is much admired, especially with regard to company culture and innovation.

Virgin operated as a private company between 1970 and 1986 when it listed on the London Stock Exchange. Richard Branson felt that public listing obligations and pressure to create short-term profits did not suit the business, so he took the company back into private ownership. The private conglomerate model supports long-termism, healthy cross-fertilization within the group and allows the parts—and the whole—to flourish on their own terms.

Virgin's strong corporate culture is much admired, and despite not paying top salaries, Virgin is often employer of choice due to its culture of empowerment, respect and innovation. With the exception of its health-clubs operations, Virgin is not the market leader in its business fields. It aspires to do things well rather than to dominate, and has myriad competitors due to its wide diversity.

Recent trends have reinforced the effectiveness and importance of Virgin's decentralized structure. It bucked the trend over the last fifteen years, when others pursued centralization, and has proven to be better placed in today's globalized, interdependent and volatile world economy.

Virgin believes in the "power of entrepreneurship and innovation to help us rise to the new challenges that we all face."[11] There is also a strong belief that success is in the hands of employees; they are the eyes and ears due to their customer interface, they are the visible face of the brand, and they have the intellectual capacity to innovate for the future.

Virgin appears to recognize major challenges lying ahead (such as peak oil and climate change) and is acting as a force for change insofar as it can. It is also seeking alternatives and other remedial measures, but acknowledges that action in partnership is more likely to produce positive results.

The company creates resilience via diversification and is adept at moving into new business areas with innovative offerings. It targets such areas carefully and demonstrates a record of good business judgement and skillful implementation. It is true to say that Virgin is good at leveraging opportunities, but there is less evidence of Virgin being adept at creating new opportunities in the sense of first-to-market product or service innovation (the exception being Virgin Galactic, which is truly pioneering[12]).

Resilient

Virgin is deeply attuned to its external environment as it encourages all layers of the organization to operate in a networked fashion with stakeholders. This approach helps to predict and pre-empt certain environmental changes, which can then be mitigated via Virgin's innovative solutions. For example, in response to security disruptions to the airline business, Virgin identified resilience strategies, which include:

- a partnership approach
- openness to new ideas and methods

- dynamic learning
- confidence in decision-making processes
- empowerment.

Optimizing

Richard Branson's commitment to the decentralized, private conglomerate model (bucking both business trends and market norms) is a great example of form fitting function and has delivered benefits over the years. Virgin has a low business failure rate and relatively high spend per head on recruitment and people development. "Contrary to what some people may think, our constantly expanding and eclectic empire is neither random nor reckless. Each successive venture demonstrates our devotion to picking the right market and the right opportunity."[13]

Adaptive

There is no single management or organizational style within Virgin. Instead many varied styles and approaches are used in different contexts. The group describes itself as a "venture capital organization," which embodies its innovative spirit and willingness to push boundaries.

Both Virgin Rail and Virgin Atlantic have invested in the use of biofuels and made innovative inroads into rail and flight journeys running on a mix of renewable fuels. In 2011, Virgin Atlantic announced a "breakthrough" fuel that will provide half the life-cycle carbon footprint of normal aviation fuel. Virgin Atlantic is helping to pioneer a method of capturing waste gases from industrial steel production, which are then fermented and chemically converted for use as a jet fuel. We can see here the opportunity of industrial symbiosis, such as in partnering with Tata Steel mentioned in the previous case study.

Systems-based

"We are a community, with shared ideas, values, interests and goals. The proof of our success is real and tangible."[14] The organization has established an internal communications community. The Virgin Village is a Group intranet site where employees are able to access information about the company, job opportunities, contacts and so on.

Our companies are part of a family rather than a hierarchy. They are empowered to run their own affairs, yet the companies help one another, and solutions to problems often come from within the Group somewhere. In a sense we are a commonwealth, with shared ideas, values, interests and goals.[15]

Often Virgin's expansion into new markets has been through a series of joint ventures whereby Virgin provided the brand and expertise and its partner provided the majority of capital (e.g., Virgin Direct and Virgin Mobile). The internal ecosystem thus merges with the external ecosystem.

Values-led

Virgin is a great example of a values-led culture. Leadership teams are built around mutual respect for each other's talents. The former CEO of Virgin Blue (now Virgin Australia), Brett Godfrey, says that it's very difficult to restructure culture if people's enthusiasm or commitment has been damaged; for this reason they support the culture at all levels and spend more than industry average on recruiting people with the right value base.

The big secret to our unique Virgin culture is simple — there is no secret. We just know that creating and maintaining our enviable culture is all about infusing our core values into everything we do — we get that right and the Virgin culture just flows. Our culture is unique — we know it, we're proud of it and we work hard to make it a reality.[16]

Richard Branson is famous for encouraging his employees to use their intuition to make decisions rather than following a formal process. Employees are viewed as Virgin's greatest asset; as such, management believes that employees should be treated with respect. Management looks after their employees' welfare and allows them the freedom to flourish and be themselves. Virgin actively encourages personal expression, whether it is in their speech, creative and conceptual thinking or dress code. It is these fundamental values and beliefs that have allowed

Virgin to thrive in such competitive environments, challenge new opportunities and excel in its markets, while still continuing to operate
with integrity.

The devolved family of companies each have their own organizational approach, yet all share the overall family values summed up by
"excelling customer value." People are put first, and by putting employees first, employees are motivated and best able to put customers
first; this way customer excellence is achieved.

One such values-led group initiative is the Star Awards, where employees nominate other employees for their contribution to initiatives
that in some way inspire others or have a star quality. This helps communicate inspiration and innovative behavior across the family of companies, while also encouraging people to nominate others and promote
positive, inspiring behavior in others.

Life-supporting

Virgin's values have a strong social and environmental ethos. It is an employer of choice and targets the consumer's experience as one of its key
drivers. The group is eco-aware, but the reality is that some of its companies operate in environmentally damaging industries — most notably
its air travel and rail businesses. Efforts are being made to operate as re-
sponsibly as possible in the short to medium term, while alternatives
emerge. For example, biofuel use is being actively explored by Virgin
Atlantic, Virgin Australia and Virgin America. The Carbon War Room
initiative is (like other initiatives and companies within the group) quite
separate, yet interconnected to the group. It is an independent non-
profit organization (under the Virgin Unite umbrella) providing synergies to other parts of the group on carbon-reduction initiatives. Virgin
Unite seeks to apply the entrepreneurial might of the Virgin family to
social and environmental initiatives across the globe.

> Today Virgin Unite focuses mainly on three things: working with
> our three hundred businesses so that they put driving change
> at their very core, the incubation of new approaches to global
> leadership, like The Elders and the Carbon War Room, and the

building of a community of people that never accepts the unacceptable. Across all our businesses, we are still learning every day about how we can do better and are fully aware we are far from perfect.

— RICHARD BRANSON[17]

The group recognizes that life-supporting sustainable responsibilities vary depending on the individual company and also on the roles and responsibilities of each person across the group. The group is exploring how each organization and the family of organizations can focus on strengthening the ways products and services can provide a credible contribution to sustainable lifestyles.

Questions

1. Can you think of any organizations similar to yours that provide inspiration for you?

2. Does your organization engage with other businesses to share experiences? Could it do more of this? How could you help facilitate this?

3. Can you think of five organizations that would be good for your organization to share stories on transformation with? Why these? What in particular interests you about them?

4. Imagine your company has begun its transformation and is selected as a case study for being on the journey toward a firm of the future. What would that case study say that is unique to your business and the transformational aspects being undertaken to positively move it forward?

5. You are bright, you work hard, you are progressive and you can envision the firm of the future. List three things you can do today, within a week, within a month and within a year to drive your organization's transformation toward becoming a firm of the future.

Conclusions

If you want to see a miracle,
be the miracle.

— Bruce Almighty

Be the change

While it may appear an immense challenge to change our behavior, it is pertinent to recognize that some humans have lived and behaved (and still do live and behave) in a way that is conducive to life on Earth for the short, medium and long term. It is simply that our main ethos and approach to life has been swept up in the prevailing business paradigm — change the business paradigm and you go a long way to addressing the root cause of our many pressing challenges. Transformation of our individual beliefs and behaviors goes hand in hand with transforming our business paradigm — the two synergizing each other's transformation. As we start to look inward, within ourselves, and let go of egotistic, detached and unsustainable behaviors, replacing them with behaviors closer to our heart, we also become more content at a deeper level. In so doing, we consume less and live in ways that are mutually beneficial for ourselves and the world around us. Now that is a synergy worth striving for.

Only we, and our attitude to business, can solve the pressing challenges now facing us. The complexity of our interconnected world also has a beautiful simplicity to it — if you follow the golden rule "love thy neighbor as thyself" (neighbor not limited to just human neighbor but all parts of our interconnected web of life), then life becomes well again. The challenge with this simple solution to the root cause of our problems again lies in our own making. The challenge with "love thy neighbor as thyself" is that if one seeks to better oneself, to grow and flourish (innate qualities of life), how does one do that without incurring expense to other parts of our interconnected web of life? After all, do we not need to consume to live, to take from one source to give to ourselves and others? We can look to nature for inspiration, and we can find answers in our own human nature, deep within our own selves. Each action and interaction, if based on completeness of truth and integrity, can enable the self to grow while also being truly sustainable for the self and all neighbors.

We do not need to change as a whole species; we just need to change as individuals, as business people, as authentic humans true to ourselves and our neighbors. In turn, we inspire others; we become the change we wish to see by starting with "the person in the mirror." Turning greedy business into good business sense is the challenge and opportunity, and the good news is, it comes naturally to us upon becoming our true selves and being true to business. Those that learn to follow their true path shall be able to adapt and transform themselves and so the organizations and communities within which they operate. Those that remain incomplete and false (not rising to their true nature) will find it increasingly difficult to get away with benefiting themselves at the expense of others. This is humanity's evolution in the making, and each of us is an active co-creator in this evolution. You choose: do you help or hinder? Do you hurt or heal?

> Those businesses that do well by doing good are the ones that will thrive in the coming decades. Those that continue with "business as usual," focused solely on profit maximization, will not be around for long (and don't deserve to be).
> — RICHARD BRANSON[1]

Natural business

"Nature's business principles" do not seek to reduce organizational behavior to biology; rather, they suggest a set of behaviors and qualities that simply echo the law of the system — Earth — upon which our lives and our businesses depend. They recognize the complexity of human nature and nurture, and are neither a model nor a theory, but rather a philosophy that reminds us that while humans are a special species on

Earth, we are still part of nature and subject to its law. If we do not conduct our business within the constraints of the system, we will inevitably go out of business.

Good business sense is creative, fun and opportunistic. Good business sense improves the individual, the organization and the wider stakeholder community and environment. The daunting challenge of becoming a firm of the future can become an exciting opportunity; a path that once found becomes the only right path to follow.

There is indeed a significant gap between nature's business principles and our current prevailing business practices, rooted in our scientific and cultural heritage, as well as in our human nature, which gives us the freedom to break the rules of nature and learn (or not) accordingly. In that regard, "nature's business principles" may appear idealistic. But is there an alternative?

Biomimicry as a school of thought suggests that we can learn to play by the rules of nature, which offer a very rich source of inspiration to challenge our current unsustainable business practices and invent new strategies.[2] "Nature's business principles" are universal, but there is room for specific individual behaviors, and indeed we as individuals and businesspeople need to invent our future in a great variety of ways. We ought to accept that we are stepping into the unknown and let go of the need to find an answer or singular goal to achieve. We should rather recognize that we are on a journey not toward the optimal organization or business model, but toward the understanding of business as dynamic, emergent, constantly interacting, adapting and morphing to maintain right balance and right relationship in an ever-changing environment.

> The new opportunity is to emulate nature, because in so doing, we bring our actions in alignment with our potential. We begin to get the design right. And as we get the design right, we create pathways through which new capacities, new innovations, new value can flow.
>
> — TACHI KIUCHI AND BILL SHIREMAN[3]

In these challenging (yet pivotal) times for business and humanity, we must realize that to become truly sustainable, human and business life has to become scientifically inspired, emotionally connected and spiritually entwined with nature and Gaia. Nature and business (as with nature and humanity) must be symbiotic and operate in mutualism for there to be anything resembling a successful outcome. The sooner business realizes the opportunities that come with being connected to and inspired by nature, the better for humanity, and for all species.

> Gratitude for the bounty of Nature and gratitude for the opportunities coming our way to fulfil our highest potential as human beings by learning to live in abundant harmony with her.
> — VICTOR LEBOW[4]

The path

Both the community (business ecosystem) and the individual are emergent living wholes, which have interconnected destinies. These destinies are open and not predefined, and yet when found, they resonate with life-giving energy.

You know when you are on your individual or collective right path because life conspires to help you — you feel like you are swimming with the stream rather than against it. This is where synchronicity enters your life and you become consciously aware, like a veil being lifted from your senses. Doors open for you, as if the path ahead is subtly lit for you to follow while remaining true to yourself and your environment. We have all experienced times when (perhaps even daily or weekly) things seem to just fall into place, a chance meeting solves a challenge, a strong feeling of clarity, immense emotional warmth, and so on. These are moments when reciprocity becomes woven into the interactions and the relationships become mutually beneficial, if only for that brief moment — each party benefiting in some way that may not always be apparent at first glance (sometimes the complete value of the reciprocity only fully recognized with hindsight and distance).

Good growth

In recent years, sustainable business has been dogged by "no growth" phenomena. Pointing the finger of blame for our ills at growth per se is over-simplistic at best; at worst it undermines the progress of humanity, potentially limiting the creative life force needed to positively transform.

Life is about growth, evolution and the realization of potential. Humanity's immediate learning is far deeper than simply limiting a current prevailing growth paradigm through stagnation or economic decline. It is not that growth is bad; it is the type of growth that can be bad, or good, for that matter. It is "good growth" and good business sense that need to be fed and encouraged, with bad, exploitative growth starved at source (through our own values and behaviors). Just as good human behavior can be encouraged, good growth can be positively encouraged through a focus on right qualities and quantities.

Business performance mechanisms, for example, through the use of holistic KPIs (social, environmental and economic) and integrated business reporting (to measure and then track progress over time), can greatly assist. Just as important is the positive encouragement of good growth through qualitative, more intangible ways; for example, promoting inspiring examples of good business behavior where holistic value is created, or facilitating open group forums for diverse stakeholders to share stories of how to emulate good growth, sharing the learnings, the failings and the successes in a mutually beneficial way. This balance of quantification and qualification is important in ensuring shoots of good growth are identified and nourished accordingly. As HRH The Prince of Wales has said: "Let's inspire people with positive messages about what they can start doing, not what they have to stop doing."[5]

Authenticity

The journey toward a firm of the future is as much about individual transformation as it is about organizational transformation, each being interconnected with the other. No man is an island, and no organization can thrive disconnected. In the same regard, this personal and organizational transformation is about being authentic, and true to your values and value; the authentic self and the authentic organization go hand in hand.

Finding our authentic self and organization is transformative and emergent—life, in its beautiful way, is dynamic, continually giving us opportunities to learn and grow. It is our choice, our perception and our state of mind that decide whether we become burdened by fear, anger, guilt and laziness, or whether we take each step with positivity, faith, hope and courage. This is the same for the high-performing team, the community of stakeholders, the organization and its wider business ecosystem. Be the change you wish to see — take ownership and responsibility for how you want to be — act and provide value in the world as best you can. Only then can real progress toward a firm of the future be made; an organization that not only seeks to limit its negativity on society and the environment, but also gives and in return receives, and provides net positive value enhancement to all its stakeholders and wider business environment. This is the future, and it is bright.

Love

Love has only been mentioned a couple of times in this book up until now (unlike sustainability, evolution, change and transformation, which have been mentioned countless times). Yet, without love, sustainability, evolution, change and transformation are empty. Love is what enables us to give to ourselves and others.

Love is mutually beneficial and always creates conditions conducive to life — love feeds on and grows from love. It breeds virtuous cycles. Leadership and organizations of the future are more about love than profit — now here is a new business paradigm in the making, and one that does not need an "ism."

> Where love rules, there is no will to power; where power predominates, there love is lacking. The one is the shadow of the other.
> — CARL JUNG[6]

If we are to be successful in transforming ourselves, our organizations and economies, then the steps of change we take need to resonate with love to ensure the outcomes of our interventions are complete and wholly beneficial: love for ourselves, our neighbors and the wider web of life. Learning to love ourselves and the rich tapestry of life is perhaps the greatest challenge and opportunity that lie ahead on our transformative journey.

Notes

These notes can also be found online, with clickable links to the web addresses: see greenbooks.co.uk/natureofbusiness

Preface
This "setting the scene" section was co-created with Louise Carver. In this section we have drawn on the following publications, listed in the Further Reading section: Capra (2002), Escobar (1996), Foster (1997), McGilchrist (2009), Sullivan (2008) and Tarnas (1991).

Module One

1. Fractional Reserve Banking definition from en.wikipedia.org/wiki /Fractional_reserve_banking.
2. The *Daily Telegraph* report on a speech in Liverpool by Sir Mervyn King, 21 October 2011. See telegraph.co.uk/finance/financialcrisis/8848051 /Mervyn-King-time-running-out-to-solve-world-economy-crisis.html.
3. See brainyquote.com/quotes/authors/a/albert_einstein.html.
4. Hawken, P. (2007) *Blessed Unrest*. New York: Penguin Group.
5. See jonathansapir.sys-con.com.
6. See en.wikipedia.org/wiki/Six_Sigma.
7. McGilchrist, I. (2010). "The Divided Brain and the Making of the Western World." RSA lecture. See youtube.com/watch?v=SbUHxC4wiWk.
8. See thinkexist.com/quotation/the_intuitive_mind_is_a_sacred_gift _and_the/15585.html.
9. McGilchrist, I. (2010). RSA lecture.
10. See sys-think.com.
11. See bethechange.org.uk.
12. Vance, D. (2009). "Nike and Sustainability" presentation, AMR Research's Sustainability Exchange 2009, Boston, MA, November.
13. Sull, D. (2009). *The Upside of Turbulence*. London: HarperCollins, p. 22.
14. See nikeinc.com/pages/responsibility.
15. Mohandas K. Gandhi. Quoted in Schumacher, E. F. (1973), *Small Is Beautiful: A Study of Economics as if People Mattered*. London: Blond & Briggs.
16. Quoted in Tata Services (2010), *A Journey Towards An Ideal*. Mumbai: Tata

Services Ltd, p. 25. Available from csridentity.com/tata/A%20Journey%20
Towards%20an%20Ideal.pdf.

17. Hawken, P., Lovins, A. and Lovins, H. (1999). *Natural Capitalism*. London: Earthscan.

18. Branson, R. (2011). *Screw Business As Usual*. London: Virgin Books, p. 217.

19. Taleb, N. N. (2007). *The Black Swan*. London: Allen Lane.

Module Two

This module was co-created with Denise Deluca, co-founder and Director of BCI.

1. Braungart, M. and McDonough, W. (2009). *Cradle to Cradle: Re-making the Way We Make Things*. London: Vintage, p. 120.

2. Hooper, J. and Teresi, D. (1986). *The 3-Pound Universe*. London: Macmillan, p. 375.

3. Benyus, J. (2002). *Biomimicry: Innovation Inspired by Nature*. New York: Harper Perennial.

4. Capra, F. (2003). *The Hidden Connections: A Science for Sustainable Living*. London: Flamingo, p. 202.

5. Ibid., p. 7.

6. Adapted from the list at biomimicryinstitute.org/downloads/LP_list.pdf.

7. See laptopmag.com/review/laptops/best-of-ces-2010.aspx?pid=14.

8. See biomimicryinstitute.org/case-studies/case-studies/transportation.html.

9. See asknature.org/product/373ec79cd6dba791bc00ed32203706a1.

10. See asknature.org/product/2a4684ab51bc3f3dfa19226d27affae3.

11. See interfaceflor.com/Default.aspx?Section=3&Sub=11.

12. See regenenergy.co.uk.

13. Kiuchi, T. and Shireman, B. (2002). *What We Learned in the Rainforest*. San Francisco, CA: Berrett-Koehler Publishers, p. 221.

14. See businessinspiredbynature.com/bci-green-papers.

15. Ibid.

16. Ward, H. (2009). "Dow Chemicals and sustainability" presentation, AMR Research's Sustainability Exchange 2009, Boston, MA, November.

17. Deluca, T., Deluca, D. and Hutchins, G. (2010). *Firm of the Future: Inspired by Soils*. Available from businessinspiredbynature.com/bci-green-papers.

18. See money.cnn.com/magazines/fortune/bestcompanies/2009/snapshots/1.html.

19. Harding, S. (2009). *Animate Earth*. Totnes: Green Books, Ch. 8.

20. Stamets, P. (2005). *Mycelium Running: How Mushrooms Can Help Save the World*. Berkeley, CA: Ten Speed Press, p. 7.

21. Bonabeau, E. and Meyer, C. (2001). "Swarm Intelligence: A Whole New Way to Think About Business." *Harvard Business Review*, 1 May, p. 108.

22. Ibid., p. 113.

23. Ibid.

24. See virgin.com/about-us.

25. Kiuchi, T. and Shireman, B. (2002), pp. 116–18.

26. Zakomurnaya, E. (2007). "Semco SA: Brazilian Miracle Where Employees Set Their Salaries and Sleep in Hammocks." *Good2Work*, 8 August. See good2work.com/article/5487.

27. See peacefromharmony.org/?cat=en_c&key=477.

28. Doczi, G. (1981). *The Power of Limits*. Boston, MA: Shambhala Publications, p. 2.

29. Ibid., p. 1.

30. Lovins, H. (2011). Speech at Tomorrow's Natural Business event, London, 11 November.

31. HRH The Prince of Wales, Juniper, T. and Skelly, I. (2010). *Harmony: A New Way of Looking At Our World*. London: Blue Door.

32. For example, the *Journal of Industrial Ecology* is devoted to the subject. See yale.edu/jie.

33. Ellen Macarthur Foundation. See ellenmacarthurfoundation.org/about /circular-economy.

34. Braungart, M. and McDonough, W. (2009). *Cradle to Cradle: Re-making the Way We Make Things*. London: Vintage, p. 78.

35. Benyus, J. (2002). *Biomimicry: Innovation Inspired By Nature*. New York: Harper Perennial, p. 259.

36. See en.wikipedia.org/wiki/Kalundborg_Eco-industrial_Park.

37. See dothegreenthing.com/blog/cardboard_to_caviar.

38. Capra, F. (2003). *The Hidden Connections: A Science for Sustainable Living*. London: Flamingo, p. 104.

39. Gunderson, L. H. and Holling, C. S. (2001). *Panarchy: Understanding Transformations in Human and Natural Systems*. Washington, DC: Island Press.

40. See resalliance.org/index.php/adaptive_cycle.

41. See peopleandplace.net/perspectives/2009/1/26/collapse_and_renewal.

42. Gunderson, L. H. and Holling, C. S., p. 338.

43. Kiuchi, T. and Shireman, B., p. 146.

44. See nokia.com/global/about-nokia/company/about-us/story/the-nokia -story.

45. This section was co-created with Paul Francis, Founder of Therapeutic Shamanism. See therapeutic-shamanism.co.uk.

46. Taylor, S. (2005). *The Fall*. Alresford: O Books.

47. Harner, M. (1980). *The Way of the Shaman*. London: HarperOne.

48. See innocentdrinks.co.uk/us/being-sustainable.

49. See therapeutic-shamanism.co.uk/what%20is%20soul%20loss.html.

50. Luther Standing Bear, Chief of the Oglala, Lakota (1868–1939). See indigenouspeople.net/standbea.htm.

Module Three

1. Branson, R. (2011). *Screw Business As Usual.* London: Virgin Books, p. 96.
2. Extract from *Management Today* interview by Andrew Saunders, 1 March 2011. See managementtoday.co.uk/features/1055793/MT-Interview-Paul -Polman-Unilever.
3. International Integrated Reporting Committee. (2011). *Towards Integrated Reporting: Communicating Value in the 21st Century*, p. 11. Available from theiirc.org/wp-content/uploads/2011/09/IR-Discussion-Paper-2011 _spreads.pdf.
4. See teebweb.org.
5. TEEB. (2010). *The Economics of Ecosystems and Biodiversity: Mainstreaming the Economics of Nature: A Synthesis of the Approach, Conclusions and Recommendations of TEEB.* Available from teebweb.org/LinkClick.aspx?file ticket=bYhDohL_TuM%3D.
6. Porritt, J. (2007). *Capitalism as if the World Matters.* London: Earthscan, pp. 135–210.
7. Hopwood, A., Unerman, J. and Fries, J. (2010). *Accounting for Sustainability: Practical Insights.* London: Earthscan. See also accountingforsustain ability.org.
8. Dargent, E. (2010–2011). "Biomimicry for Business?" Final MBA dissertation, University of Exeter Business School, Exeter, UK.
9. Moore, J. (1993). "Predators and Prey: A New Ecology of Competition." *Harvard Business Review*, May, p. 77.
10. Kiuchi, T. and Shireman, B. (2002). *What We Learned in the Rainforest.* San Francisco, CA: Berrett-Koehler Publishers, p. 205.
11. These theories (and some of their principal proponents) include: *total quality management (TQM)* — Dr W. Edwards Deming and Dr J. M. Juran; *lean* — James P. Womack and Daniel Jones; *learning/holographic organizations* — Peter Senge and Gareth Morgan; *business ecosystems* — James F. Moore, Marco Iansiti and Roy Levien, as well as Adam Brandenburger and Barry J. Nalebuff with "*co-opetition*"; *innovation* — Clayton Christensen, Eric von Hippel and John Bessant; *sustainable supply chain management theory (SSCM)* — Craig R. Carter, Dale S. Rogers, Mark Pagell and Zhao-hui Wu, and more recently Michael E. Porter and Mark R. Kramer with "*shared value*"; *core competence, strategic intent, evolving capabilities* — Gary Hamel, C. K. Prahalad, Robert H. Hayes and Gary P. Pisano; *management by values* — Rosabeth Moss Kanter and Morgen Witzel; *natural capitalism, cradle-to-cradle* and *solution-based* business models — Paul Hawken, Amory Lovins, Hunter Lovins, William McDonough and Michael Braungart.
12. See ge.com/uk/company/ecomagination/index.html/
13. See novonordisk.co.uk/documents/promotion_page/document/2_about _us.asp.
14. Holliday, C., Schmidheiny, S. and Watts, P. (2002). *Walking the Talk: The*

Business Case for Sustainable Development. Sheffield: Greenleaf Publishing, p. 156.

15. Ibid., p. 157.

16. Lubin, D. A. and Esty, D. C. (2010). "The Sustainability Imperative." *Harvard Business Review*, May, p. 48.

17. Pagell, M. and Wu, Z. (2009). "Building a More Complete Theory of Sustainable Supply Chain Management Using Case Studies of 10 Exemplars." *Journal of Supply Chain Management*, vol. 45, no. 2, April, pp. 50–2.

18. Porter, M. and Kramer, M. (2011). "Creating Shared Value." *Harvard Business Review*, January–February, pp. 62–77.

19. Panasonic. (2011). *Sustainability Report 2011*. Tokyo, Japan: Panasonic Corporation. Available from web panasonic.net/csr/reports.

20. See wholefoodsmarket.com/values/sustainability.php#1.

21. Porritt, J., p. 314.

22. Braungart, M. and McDonough, W. (2009). *Cradle to Cradle: Re-making the Way We Make Things*. London: Vintage, p. 16.

Module Four

1. See novonordisk.co.uk/documents/article_page/document/about_us_sustainability.asp.

2. Porritt, J. (2007). *Capitalism as if the World Matters*. London: Earthscan, p. 194.

3. These system conditions have been summarized by The Natural Step as "digging, dumping, destroying and demeaning." naturalstep.org/en/the-four-system-conditions.

4. Nattrass, B. and Altomare, M. (1999). *The Natural Step for Business*, Stockholm: The Natural Step.

5. See skanska.co.uk/About-Skanska/Sustainability.

6. Anderson, R. and White, R. (2009). *Confessions of a Radical Industrialist*. New York: Random House Business Books.

7. See ceres.org/company-network/how-we-work-with-companies/performance.

8. See nikebiz.com/crreport/content/about/2-1-0-ceo-letter.php.

9. See atkearney.com/index.php/News-media/companies-with-a-commitment-to-sustainability-tend-to-outperform-their-peers-during-the-financial-crisis.html.

10. See bitc.org.uk/resources/publications/the_value_of.html.

11. Branson, R. (2011). *Screw Business As Usual*. London: Virgin Books, p. 41.

12. Ibid., p. 18.

13. Nayar, V. (2010). *Employees First, Customers Second: Turning Conventional Management Upside Down*. Boston, MA: Harvard Business School Publishing.

14. See johnlewispartnership.co.uk/about/our-constitution.html.

15. Branson, R., p. 50.
16. Holliday, C., Schmidheiny, S. and Watts, P. (2002). *Walking the Talk: The Business Case for Sustainable Development*. Sheffield: Greenleaf Publishing, p. 103.
17. Ibid., p. 128.
18. de Botton, A. (2004). *Status Anxiety*. London: Penguin Books.
19. Tata Services. (2010). *A Journey Towards An Ideal*. Mumbai: Tata Services Ltd, p. 98. Available from csridentity.com/tata/A%20Journey%20Towards%20an%20Ideal.pdf.
20. Porter, M. and Kramer, M. (2011). "Creating Shared Value." *Harvard Business Review*, January–February, pp. 62–77.
21. Porter, M. (2011). The UBS Q-Series: Sustainable Innovation and Growth Conference. New York, 19 October.
22. See www.toyota-global.com/company/vision_philosophy/guiding _principles.html.
23. jnj.com/connect/about-jnj/jnj-credo.
24. Contribution from Veronica Heaven of The Heaven Company. See heavencompany.com.
25. Hawken, P., Lovins, A. and Lovins, H. (1999). *Natural Capitalism*. London: Earthscan, p. 134.
26. Baines, T. S., Lightfoot, H. W., Benedettini, O. and Kay, J. M. (2009). "The Servitization of Manufacturing: A Review of Literature and Reflection on Future Challenges." *Journal of Manufacturing Technology Management*, vol. 20, no. 5, pp. 547–67.
27. Hawken, P., Lovins, A. and Lovins, H., p. 143.
28. See interfaceflor.co.uk/web/our_services/tile_take_back.
29. Evans, S., Bergendahl, M. N., Gregory, M. and Ryan, C. (2009). *Towards a Sustainable Industrial System: Accelerating the Contribution of Education and Research*. Cambridge: University of Cambridge Institute for Manufacturing and Cranfield University, p. 13. Available from ifm.eng.cam.ac.uk/sis/indus trial_sustainability_report.pdf.
30. See industrialsustainability.org.
31. Contribution from Jon Allen of Jon Allen Architect. See jonallenarchitect .co.uk.
32. Whitefield, P. (1993). *Permaculture in a Nutshell*. East Meon: Permanent Publications.
33. See transitionculture.org/2008/12/18/david-holmgren-on-permaculture -business-resilience-and-transition.
34. Atos. (2011). *Journey 2014 — Simplicity with Control*. London: Atos International.
35. Porritt, J., p. 161.
36. Lovins, A. B., Lovins, L. H. and Hawken, P. (1999). "A Road Map for Natural Capitalism." *Harvard Business Review*, May–June, p. 148.

Module Five

1. Lipton, B. (2008). *The Biology of Belief*. Carlsbad, CA: Hay House. Lipton, B. and Bhaerman, S. (2009). *Spontaneous Evolution*. Carlsbad, CA: Hay House.
2. Jones, P. (2011). "Steps Towards Happiness." *Resurgence*, no. 269, November–December, p. 40.
3. Marks, N. (2011). "Creating a Well-being Society." Ibid., p. 22.
4. Senge, P. M., Scharmer, C. O., Jaworski, J. and Flowers, B. S. (2004). *Presence: Human Purpose and the Field of the Future*. London: Nicholas Brealey, p. 216.
5. Hemming, H. (2011). *Together: How Small Groups Achieve Big Things*. London: John Murray Publishers, p. 237.
6. Kiuchi, T. and Shireman, B. (2002). *What We Learned in the Rainforest*. San Francisco, CA: Berrett-Koehler Publishers, p. 119.
7. Deming, W. E. (2000). *Out of the Crisis*. Cambridge, MA: MIT Press.
8. Dargent, E. (2010–2011). "Biomimicry for Business?" Final MBA dissertation, University of Exeter Business School, Exeter, UK, p. 39.
9. Morgan, G. (1997). *Images of Organizations*. London: Sage Publications, p. 106. Hayes, R. H. and Pisano, G. P. (1994). "Beyond World-class Manufacturing." *Harvard Business Review*, January–February, pp. 77–86.
10. Senge, P. (1993). *The Fifth Discipline: The Art and Practice of the Learning Organization*. New York: Doubleday Currency.
11. Ibid.
12. Tata Services. (2010). *A Journey Towards An Ideal*. Mumbai: Tata Services Ltd, p. 6. Available from csridentity.com/tata/A%20Journey%20Towards %20an%20Ideal.pdf.
13. Kiuchi, T. and Shireman, B., p. 159.
14. Ibid., p. 160.
15. Tata Services, p. 6. Available fromcsridentity.com/tata/A%20Journey%20 Towards%20an%20Ideal.pdf.
16. See biomimicry-bci.squarespace.com/blog/2012/2/22/leadership-inspired -by-nature-redesigning-for-resilience.html.
17. Capra, F. (2003). *The Hidden Connections: A Science for Sustainable Living*. London: Flamingo, pp. 106–12.
18. See imaginiz.com/provocative/change/semco.html.
19. See danone.com/?lang=en.
20. This section was co-created with Alfred Schmits, Founder of The Conscious Company. See theconsciouscompany.com.
21. Mr Manish Vaidya, General Manager, Climate Change Cluster, Tata Quality Management Services. In Tata Services (2010), *A Journey Towards An Ideal*. Mumbai: Tata Services Ltd, p. 39. Available from csridentity.com/tata /A%20Journey%20Towards%20an%20Ideal.pdf.
22. Ray Anderson, former Chairman and CEO of InterfaceFLOR. In Anderson,

R. and White, R. (2009), *Confessions of a Radical Industrialist*. New York: Random House Business Books, p. 7.

23. This section was co-created with Mike Edwards, founder of IndigeNouse. See indigenouse.co.uk.

24. This section was co-created with Peter Redstone, co-founder of Barefoot Thinking. See barefoot-thinking.com.

25. Kline, N. (1999). *Time To Think: Listening to Ignite the Human Mind*. London: Cassell.

26. de Bono, E. (2004). *Edward de Bono's Thinking Course*. London, BBC Books; Buzan, T. (2002). *How to Mind Map: The Ultimate Thinking Tool That Will Change Your Life*. London: Thorsons.

27. Sawyer, K. (2008). *Group Genius — The Creative Power of Collaboration*. New York: Basic Books.

28. See benfurman.com.

29. See scientificamerican.com/article.cfm?id=building-around-the-mind.

30. Serrat, O. (2009). "Exercising Servant Leadership." *Knowledge Solutions*, no. 63, September. Available from adb.org/documents/information /knowledge-solutions/exercising-servant-leadership.pdf.

31. Kline, N. (1999). *Time To Think: Listening to Ignite the Human Mind*. London: Cassell, p. 37.

32. See brief.org.uk/view.php?item_id=108.

33. Sull, D. (2009). *The Upside of Turbulence*. New York: HarperCollins, p. 145.

Module Six

1. Nowak, M. and Highfield, R. (2011). *Super Cooperators: Evolution, Altruism and Human Behavior, or Why We Need Each Other to Succeed*. Edinburgh: Canongate, p. xvii.

2. Hickman, L. (2011). "Trust Me." *Resurgence*, No. 269, November–December, p. 60.

3. See bbc.co.uk/news/business-15282615.

4. See innovateonpurpose.blogspot.com/2011/03/evolution-of-innovation -funnel.html.

5. Chesbrough, H. (2006). "Open Innovation: A New Paradigm for Understanding Industrial Innovation." In *Open Innovation: Researching a New Paradigm*, H. Chesbrough, W. Vanhaverbeke and J. West (eds). Oxford: Oxford University Press.

6. See innovationexchange.com.

7. See jovoto.com.

8. Schumacher, E. F. (1973). *Small Is Beautiful: A Study of Economics as if People Mattered*. London: Blond & Briggs, p. 66.

9. See mukwonagoriver.org/paul-hawken-on-social-movements.

Module Seven

This module was co-created with Denise Deluca and Andy Middleton of BCI.

1. See guardian.co.uk/sustainable-business/b-q-ceo-ian-cheshire-capitalism-reappraisal.
2. See appliedimprov.ning.com.
3. Kline, N. (1999). *Time To Think: Listening to Ignite the Human Mind*. London: Cassell, p. 36.

Module Eight

1. See bitc.org.uk.
2. Anant G. Nadkarni, Vice-President, Group Corporate Sustainability. In Tata Services (2010), *A Journey Towards An Ideal*. Mumbai: Tata Services Ltd, p. 11. Available from csridentity.com/tata/A%20Journey%20Towards%20an%20Ideal.pdf.
3. Group Chairman Ratan Tata. Ibid., p. 83. Available from csridentity.com/tata/A%20Journey%20Towards%20an%20Ideal.pdf.
4. Anant G. Nadkarni. Ibid, p. 85. Available from csridentity.com/tata/A%20Journey%20Towards%20an%20Ideal.pdf.
5. See images.businessweek.com/ss/10/04/0415_most_innovative_companies/1.htm.
6. Tata Services. (2010). *A Journey Towards An Ideal*. Mumbai: Tata Services Ltd, p. 26. Available from csridentity.com/tata/A%20Journey%20Towards%20an%20Ideal.pdf.
7. See tatacommunications.com/about/culture.asp.
8. T. R. Doongaji, former Managing Director, Tata Services and Guardian CEO, Mumbai Regional Group. In Tata Services (2010), p. 19. Available from csridentity.com/tata/A%20Journey%20Towards%20an%20Ideal.pdf.
9. Foram Nagori, Manager CS, The Taj Group of Hotels. Ibid., p. 12. Available from csridentity.com/tata/A%20Journey%20Towards%20an%20Ideal.pdf.
10. Ibid., p. 56.
11. See virgin.com/people-and-planet/our-vision.
12. See virgingalactic.com/overview.
13. See virgin.com/about-us.
14. See gbchealthstage.metarhythm.com/member_profiles/157-virgin_group.
15. See virgin.com/about-us.
16. See hcamag.com/news/profiles/breaking-in-a-new-culture-the-virgin-blue-story/110539.
17. Branson, R. (2011). *Screw Business As Usual*. London: Virgin Books, p. 125.

Module Nine

1. Branson, R. (2011). *Screw Business As Usual*. London: Virgin Books, p. 331.

2. Dargent, E. (2010–2011). "Biomimicry for Business?" Final MBA dissertation, University of Exeter Business School, Exeter, UK, p. 47.

3. Kiuchi, T. and Shireman, B. (2002). *What We Learned in the Rainforest*. San Francisco, CA: Berrett-Koehler Publishers, p. 191.

4. Victor Lebow. In *Journal of Retailing* (spring 1955), quoted in Packard, V. (1960). *The Waste Makers*. New York: David McKay, p. 24.

5. See positivenews.org.uk/2011/environment/sustainable_development /5082/royal-start-sustainable-future.

6. Carl Jung. In *The Psychology of the Unconscious* (1943). See en.wikiquote.org /wiki/Carl_Jung.

Further reading

Anderson, R. and White, R. (2009). *Confessions of a Radical Industrialist*. New York: Random House Business Books.

Benyus, J. (2002). *Biomimicry: Innovation Inspired By Nature*. New York: Harper Perennial.

Branson, R. (2011). *Screw Business As Usual*. London: Virgin Books.

Braungart, M. and McDonough, W. (2009). *Cradle to Cradle: Re-making the Way We Make Things*. London: Vintage.

Capra, F. (2003). *The Hidden Connections: A Science for Sustainable Living*. London: Flamingo.

Capra, F. and Henderson, H. (2009). "Qualitative Growth." In *The Journal of the Institute of Chartered Accountants of England and Wales*. Downloadable from ethicalmarkets.com.

Doczi, G. (1981). *The Power of Limits*. Boston, MA: Shambhala Publications.

Escobar, A. (1996). "Constructing Nature: Elements for a Poststructural Political Ecology." In *Liberation Ecologies*, R. Peet and M. Watts (eds). London: Routledge.

Foster, J. M. (1997). *Valuing Nature: Ethics, Economics and the Environment*. London: Routledge.

Hawken, P., Lovins, A. and Lovins, H. (1999). *Natural Capitalism*. London: Earthscan.

HRH The Prince of Wales, Juniper, T. and Skelly, I. (2010). *Harmony: A New Way of Looking At Our World*. London: Blue Door.

Kiuchi, T. and Shireman, B. (2002). *What We Learned in the Rainforest*. San Francisco, CA: Berrett-Koehler Publishers.

Kline, N. (1999). *Time To Think: Listening to Ignite the Human Mind*. London: Cassell.

Lipton, B. and Bhaerman, S. (2009). *Spontaneous Evolution*. Carlsbad, CA: Hay House.

Macartney, T. (2007). *Finding Earth, Finding Soul: The Invisible Path to Authentic Leadership*. Totnes: Green Books.

McGilchrist, I. (2009). *The Master and His Emissary*. New Haven, CT: Yale University Press.

Pauli, G. (1998). *Upsizing: The Road To Zero Emissions*. Sheffield: Greenleaf Publishing.

Porritt, J. (2007). *Capitalism as if the World Matters*. London: Earthscan.

Schumacher, E. F. (1973). *Small Is Beautiful: A Study of Economics as if People Mattered*. London: Blond & Briggs.

Senge, P. (1993). *The Fifth Discipline: The Art and Practice of the Learning Organization*. New York: Doubleday Currency.

Senge, P. M., Scharmer, C. O., Jaworski, J. and Flowers, B. S. (2004). *Presence: Human Purpose and the Field of the Future*. London: Nicholas Brealey.

Sullivan, S. (2008). *Markets for Biodiversity and Ecosystems: Reframing Nature for Capitalist Expansion?* London: International Institute of Environment and Development.

Tarnas, R. (1991). *The Passion of the Western Mind: Understanding the Ideas That Have Shaped Our World View*. New York: Ballantine Books.

Taylor, S. (2005). *The Fall*. Alresford: O Books.

Worldwatch Institute. (2010). *State of The World 2010: Transforming Cultures from Consumerism to Sustainability*. London: Earthscan.

Index

Page numbers in *italic* refer to Figures

About the Author

In 2009, I co-founded a collective of specialists in "Business Inspired By Nature" called Biomimicry for Creative Innovation (BCI) and, to this day, have the great pleasure of working collaboratively with some great minds in ecological thinking for business transformation. Also I globally headed up Sustainability Solutions for Atos International (an international IT services provider) and di-rectly contributed to ensuring sustainable business became a conscious part of the newly merged organization with its 75,000 employees and diverse set of international clients.

In 2010, I moved deeper in to nature (Devon in south west England) to live more simply, yet paradoxically, more richly in my view. I am undergoing a transformation on many levels; understanding how to walk my life path with courage and conviction. A key aspect of my path is reconnecting and re-enchanting myself (and others) with the diverse beauty of the world around us, while helping business and society evolve towards a sustainable future. The two, my personal life and my working life, go hand in hand symbiotically; and the fun part is there is always room for learning and improvement. In September 2012 our first child was born, Lilly-Belle, who is already well connected to nature and fortunately loves the dawn and dusk nature walks I take her on.

It is my hope that *The Nature of Business* helps repair the crucially important bridge between business and nature.

If you have enjoyed *The Nature of Business,* you might also enjoy other

Books to Build a New Society

Our books provide positive solutions for people who want to make a difference. We specialize in:

**Sustainable Living • Green Building • Peak Oil
Renewable Energy • Environment & Economy
Natural Building & Appropriate Technology
Progressive Leadership • Resistance and Community
Educational & Parenting Resources**

New Society Publishers
ENVIRONMENTAL BENEFITS STATEMENT

New Society Publishers has chosen to produce this book on recycled paper made with 100% post consumer waste, processed chlorine free, and old growth free.

For every 5,000 books printed, New Society saves the following resources:[1]

25	Trees
2,264	Pounds of Solid Waste
2,491	Gallons of Water
3,249	Kilowatt Hours of Electricity
4,115	Pounds of Greenhouse Gases
18	Pounds of HAPs, VOCs, and AOX Combined
6	Cubic Yards of Landfill Space

---

[1]Environmental benefits are calculated based on research done by the Environmental Defense Fund and other members of the Paper Task Force who study the environmental impacts of the paper industry.

For a full list of NSP's titles, please call 1-800-567-6772 *or check out our website at:*

www.newsociety.com

new society
PUBLISHERS